Diplomacy for Victory

THE NORTON ESSAYS IN AMERICAN HISTORY

Under the general editorship of

HAROLD M. HYMAN

William P. Hobby Professor of American History
Rice University

Diplomacy for Victory

FDR and Unconditional Surrender

Raymond G. O'Connor

W · W · NORTON & COMPANY · INC · *New York*

Library of Congress Catalog Card No. 70-155986

SBN 393 05441 1 Cloth Edition

SBN 393 09765 X Paper Edition

3 4 5 6 7 8 9 0

For Terry, Roy, and Denny

Contents

MAPS

Introduction

〰〰〰〰〰〰〰〰〰〰〰〰〰〰〰〰〰〰〰〰〰〰〰〰〰〰〰〰〰〰

ON JANUARY 24, 1943, President Franklin D. Roosevelt declared in a press conference at Casablanca that "The elimination of German, Japanese, and Italian war power means the unconditional surrender by Germany, Italy, and Japan." [1] Then and since the source of much controversy, this "doctrine" has been cited as evidence that the President, unlike his associate, Prime Minister Winston Churchill, conceived of the war in an exclusively military sense, ignored the political objectives inherent in the use of armed force, prolonged the conflict, and made it possible for the Soviet Union to shape the peace, dominate Eastern Europe, and threaten the security of the Western world.[2]

Contributing to this version of Roosevelt's wartime diplomacy are widely accepted interpretations of America's military ventures.[3] At the height of the debate over the Korean War, General Douglas MacArthur declared, "War's very objective is victory—not prolonged indecision. In war there is no substitute for victory." Elaborating on this theme, the General went on to say, the "new

1. Samuel I. Rosenman, ed., *1943: The Tide Turns* (*The Public Papers and Addresses of Franklin D. Roosevelt,* Vol. XII) (New York, 1950), 39.
2. For example, Hanson W. Baldwin, *Great Mistakes of the War* (New York, 1950); Chester Wilmot, *The Struggle for Europe* (New York, 1952); Anne Armstrong, *Unconditional Surrender: The Impact of the Casablanca Policy upon World War II* (New Brunswick, N.J., 1961).
3. The term *diplomacy* is employed in its broadest sense, i.e., "the management of international relations," embracing both negotiation and policy.

concept . . . which tends to disavow victory as the combat objective" stemmed from those who were "oblivious to the lessons of military history and the American tradition." Senator Barry Goldwater, sharing these sentiments, complained that "Once upon a time our traditional goal in war . . . was victory." Scholars, too, have echoed this reading of America's past, although often in a critical vein. The unconditional surrender doctrine, Anne Armstrong writes, "was Franklin Roosevelt's phrase and policy and seems to have grown naturally, perhaps inevitably, out of the American experience and the American tradition of warfare. It reflected the basic American war aim of victory." [4] Henry Kissinger found that for Americans, "war was conducted on the basis of purely military considerations; to intrude 'politics' into it was considered wrong, even immoral. Until victory was achieved the diplomats had to stand aside." [5] Within the context of these forthright expositions of the nation's record, it is little wonder that Roosevelt's diplomacy is viewed by many as inadequate, shortsighted, or virtually nonexistent.[6]

But an understanding, much less an evaluation, of the policy announced at Casablanca requires an investigation of the origins of the doctrine, the competition on the international scene which resulted in World War II, the events that led to American involvement, the peace aims of the adversaries, the conflicting military strategies, and the negotiating abilities of the heads of

4. Armstrong, *Unconditional Surrender,* 40–41. The "complementary" nature of the tasks of the soldier and the statesman apparently was destroyed in World War I, when the enormity and repercussions of the struggle caused military considerations to predominate. Gordon A. Craig, "The Revolution in War and Diplomacy, 1914–1939," in Gordon A. Craig, *War, Politics, and Diplomacy: Selected Essays* (New York, 1966), 197.
5. Henry A. Kissinger, Preface to Urz Schwartz, *American Strategy: A New Perspective* (New York, 1966), xiii.
6. See Gaddis Smith, *American Diplomacy During the Second World War* (New York, 1965); William L. Neumann, *After Victory: Churchill, Roosevelt, Stalin and the Making of the Peace* (New York, 1967); Gabriel Kolko, *The Politics of War: The World and United States Foreign Policy, 1943–1945* (New York, 1968).

state in their exchanges via communications media or at the conference table. In attempting to unravel this tangled skein, the student is confronted by an overwhelming mass of documents, memoirs, articles, and books, all with the professed object of shedding some light on this most massive of human struggles. The historian, faced with an obligation to explain as well as describe the past, cannot help being intimidated by the enormity of his task, the magnitude of the problems that confronted the leaders of the warring nations, and the obstacles that were overcome as the antagonists battled for survival.

Survival, as each government saw it, was behind all of the mobilization, bloodshed, and destruction that enveloped the globe for these six fateful years. The often-ignored dictum of the Prussian strategist Karl von Clausewitz that "war is regarded as nothing but the *continuation of state policy with other means*" was revived.[7] and the political consequences of combat assumed greater proportions as the romantic aspects of warfare were obscured by the depersonalized mechanization of mass destruction. Perhaps more clearly than before, force was perceived as the means by which vital goals could be attained. Throughout the conflict public declarations of the leading protagonists were devoted to promises of a new world order that would emerge to justify the enormous sacrifices, a world order to ensure not only peace but a variety of rights and freedoms that had widespread appeal. The sincerity of these noble pronouncements may be questioned, for moral exhortations dealing in absolutes are not uncommon among political leaders. Reinhold Niebuhr may be correct in asserting that "A modern nation does not dare to go to war for reasons other than those of self-interest and cannot conduct the war without claiming to be motivated by higher motives than those of self-interest." [8] But the fact remains that the *ends* rather than the means were given a good deal of em-

7. Karl von Clausewitz, *On War,* translated from the German by O. J. Matthijs Jolles (New York, 1942), xxix.
8. Reinhold Niebuhr, *The Children of Light and the Children of Darkness* (New York, 1953), 170.

phasis, which indicated not only that the leaders were conscious of the correlation between fighting and national policy but that the public became aware of the stakes and had high expectations. Thus the military strategy—the means—had to be coordinated with the political objectives, for the way a war is waged certainly influences, if it does not determine, the nature of the peace. And if military victory were not achieved, the entire effort would be fruitless.

The inordinate complexities of land, sea, and air hostilities were intensified by the need to coordinate efforts among the various allies. The basic problems of coalition warfare were strategic, logistic, and political. It was not simply a matter of allowing the military commanders to conduct the war as they saw fit, for too many decisions involved factors outside their control. Priorities in regard to men, materiel, and even campaigns had to be resolved by the heads of government, who in turn found themselves and their military advisers differing over substantive issues. The reconciliation of these differences, which at times threatened to break up the coalition, demanded patience, tolerance, compromise, and negotiating skill of the highest order. The success of the effort from a military standpoint was demonstrated by the defeat of the Axis Powers. But victory is composed of many ingredients, and whether the other ambitions of the Allied nations were realized is the crux of the story.

This book is the product of many minds, including those of colleagues, associates, participants in the events, and students who continue to demonstrate that learning is a reciprocal process. Although these are not reflected in the footnotes and the Bibliographic Review, the author has profited by several trips to the Franklin D. Roosevelt Library at Hyde Park, New York; and numerous explorations of pertinent materials at the National Archives; the Department of State; the Naval History Division, Department of the Navy; and the Harry S Truman Library at Independence, Missouri. The aid provided by the staffs of these depositories has been invaluable. More specifically, I want to express my thanks to Dr. William M. Franklin of the Historical Office, Department of State, and Professor Louis Morton, Dartmouth College, who read a draft of the manuscript and gave me the benefit of their suggestions; to Dr. Forrest C. Pogue, Director of the George C. Marshall Research Library, who in conversation and correspondence clarified many items; to Professor Harold M. Hyman, editor of this series, who contributed encouragement and constructive counsel. Nursing me through the intricacies of publication were James L. Mairs, editor, and Elissa Epel of W. W. Norton & Company, whose attention to detail eliminated a number of obscurities. A special note of gratitude goes to the typist, Anita Richards, whose facility for transcribing unintelligible copy is remarkable. Of course none of the aforementioned individuals bears any responsibility for errors or interpretations in the text, a prerogative reserved by precedent and fiat to the author.

Diplomacy for Victory

1

Roosevelt and the American Military Tradition

WHEN PRESIDENT ROOSEVELT contemplated the terms on which the war against the Axis powers should be terminated, he was able to call on his own and his country's experience. Historically, the United States had never demanded that the enemy surrender unconditionally in any conflicts with other nations. The American Revolution was concluded by negotiation, and when Great Britain granted the "necessary" rather than the "desirable" concessions, the fighting stopped. During the so-called Quasi-War with France, 1798–1800, when President John Adams secured congressional authority to wage naval warfare, a compromise settlement was accepted. The War of 1812 was concluded after prolonged deliberations at Ghent with none of the declared American war aims being realized. The various conflicts with the Barbary powers were ended by negotiated agreements which embodied concessions by both sides. War with Mexico found President Polk obliged to employ more force than he had anticipated, but again the peace treaty was a negotiated document.

Aside from the Indian campaigns, the domestic Civil War brought a deviation from previous American practice. Hostilities ended with, in the words of the Williams Resolution of

February 13, 1865, "the unconditional submission of those who have rebelled against us." Perhaps inspired by Grant's famous ultimatum to the commanding officer at Fort Donelson, "No terms except unconditional and immediate surrender can be accepted," the phrase aptly described the fate of the Confederate government and its troops. But a generation later the war against Spain was terminated by an armistice protocol which provided the basis for a final treaty, and peace was restored in a manner more consistent with what had been the American tradition prior to 1865.

The First World War brought Franklin Roosevelt into direct contact with the problems of war and peace. As Assistant Secretary of the Navy under Josephus Daniels from 1913 to 1920 he was intimately associated with military strategy, and he observed at first hand the use of armed force to secure political objectives. The war scare with Japan, the occupation of Vera Cruz, the employment of the Navy in Haiti and Santo Domingo, and the expedition into Mexico after Pancho Villa found him directly involved in the planning, preparation, and execution of military operations. Long an admirer of his Republican cousin Theodore's "big stick" philosophy, Roosevelt had corresponded with the sea-power exponent, Rear Admiral Alfred Thayer Mahan, and accepted many of his theories. Roosevelt shared his older cousin's impatience with President Wilson's procrastination in entering the First World War, and enthusiastically supported the American declaration of war in April 1917.

Prior to American involvement President Wilson had made several attempts to halt the carnage, and his eloquent plea of January 22, 1917, marked the culmination of his efforts. There must be a "peace without victory," Wilson contended, for "Victory would mean peace forced upon the loser, a victor's terms imposed upon the vanquished. It would be accepted in humiliation, under duress, at an intolerable sacrifice, and would leave a sting, a resentment, a bitter memory upon which terms of peace would rest, not permanently, but only as upon quicksand. Only a peace between equals can last." In spite of some criticism, the phrase "peace without victory" did catch the popular imagination, and press reaction was favorable. Unfortunately, the President's appeal was quickly lost in the rush of events that brought the United States into the war.[1]

Franklin Roosevelt publicly endorsed the idealistic motives in which Wilson clothed American intervention, and he found exhilarating the increased demands on his job in the prosecution of the war. When the first German overture for an armistice reached Washington on October 7, 1918, Roosevelt shared the widespread objections to any agreement for a cessation of hostilities that resembled a "peace without victory." From the Allies, members of Congress, and the press came reactions against some type of "conditional" peace. This attitude had been shaped in part by the President himself, most recently in an address some ten days before receipt of the German note. Rejecting "any kind of bargain or compromise with the Governments of the Central Empires," he asserted, "We cannot 'come to terms' with them," and promised "complete victory." After such a forthright, categorical declaration, it is little wonder that a violent controversy ensued when the public learned that the President was negotiating with Germany.

The chambers of Congress reverberated with speeches and resolutions suggesting how the war should be concluded. Resolutions introduced in the Senate provided for "no cessation of hostilities and no armistice until the Imperial German Government shall disband its armies and surrender its arms and munitions together with its Navy"; no negotiations "until and before such time as the German armed forces shall have surrendered"; and, from Senator Henry Cabot Lodge, "no further communication with the German Government upon the subject of an armistice or conditions of peace, except a demand for unconditional surrender." Other resolutions supported the

1. For a further discussion see Ross Gregory, *The Origins of American Intervention in the First World War* (New York, 1971).

4 Diplomacy for Victory

President's negotiations, and debate over the question continued until the armistice was announced. Outside the Congress, former President Theodore Roosevelt urged Americans to "adopt as our motto 'unconditional surrender,' " and General Pershing advised that "complete victory can only be obtained by continuing the war until we force unconditional surrender." Even an "Unconditional Surrender Club" emerged to plague the President, who felt it "unnecessary and embarrassing." Nor was the dispute confined to the President's countrymen. The European allies resisted Wilson's armistice proposals until his emissary, Colonel E. M. House, warned that the United States might withdraw from the conflict if they were not more receptive.[2]

During this period Franklin Roosevelt was directly involved in advising the President on armistice terms concerning the disposition of the German navy. Josephus Daniels, Roosevelt's chief, was actively engaged in campaigning during the crucial congressional election, and in his absence Roosevelt served as Acting Secretary. In his regular capacity he would have been aware of the controversy over the conditions to be imposed in order to terminate hostilities, but in Daniels's absence his added responsibilities made him a participant in the deliberations. Faced with a dispute among his own advisers and between the British and French governments, he recommended the surrender rather than the internment of the major portion of the German fleet. Overruling objections that such harsh terms might make the armistice unacceptable, the President followed Roosevelt's recommendation, and it was incorporated in the final document.[3]

In spite of Roosevelt's satisfaction over the naval terms of the armistice, it is likely that he shared the predilection of his older cousin and others for an unconditional surrender. Responding to a question at a press conference in 1944, Roosevelt

2. Harry R. Rudin, *Armistice, 1918* (New Haven, 1944), 266ff.
3. Frank Freidel, *The Apprenticeship* (*Franklin D. Roosevelt,* Vol. I) (Boston, 1952), 371–72; Rudin, *Armistice, 1918,* 285–319.

firmly rejected a repetition of 1918. "No," he said, "nothing like last time. That is out. That was a gift from God and General Foch. And the only man who stood out among them was General Pershing." [4] His bellicose attitude, his enthusiasm for the use of armed force, his anxiety to have the nation involved, his eager prosecution of the war, and his attitude toward the disposition of the German navy all would support his taking a hard-line position in regard to armistice terms and being dissatisfied with Wilson's negotiated and conditional approach. Later, he probably found himself in agreement with the conclusion of General Tasker H. Bliss, American representative on the Supreme War Council and a member of the delegation to the peace conference. "The one great error in the armistice, as now admitted by thinking men generally in Europe," wrote Bliss in 1922, "was in the failure to demand complete surrender with resulting disarmament and demobilization." [5] Although not directly associated with the deliberations at Versailles in 1919, Roosevelt was in Paris at the time supervising naval demobilization in Europe. As an interested and involved onlooker he had some appreciation of the knotty problems created by the inconclusive armistice agreement. As his party's vice-presidential candidate in 1920 he was drawn into the controversy over the treaty, and as a devoted student of international affairs in the following decade he was able to form strong convictions about the conflict, the way it ended, and the immediate and long-term results. While it is impossible to determine the amount of influence this direct and indirect experience exerted on Roosevelt, it must have been considerable. Obviously it had some effect on his determination to avoid a repetition of what he considered a mistake when he found himself occupying a role comparable to Wilson's in an even more catastrophic world conflagration.

4. August 15, 1944, *FDR Press Conferences,* microfilm, roll 12, vol. 24, frames 50–51.
5. Tasker H. Bliss, "The Armistice," *American Journal of International Law,* XVI (1922), 520.

So the essential point, he realized, was not merely how to stop hostilities, but to do so in a way that would facilitate the drafting and implementation of the most desirable peace terms. Wars were waged, Roosevelt knew, in order to secure national objectives, and however noble or exhilarating some might find warfare, it must be regarded as a means to the higher end of self-interest. During the period of disillusionment following America's first crusade in Europe, a common saying held that "the United States never lost a war or won a peace." Although historically inaccurate, the phrase gained widespread popularity and reflected a rejection of what many considered Wilson's obsession with world organization. Roosevelt himself was fully converted to support for the League of Nations Covenant after a conversation with the President when returning from Europe in 1919 on the same ship. During the 1920 campaign the Democratic vice-presidential candidate appeared to be a mild reservationist while urging approval of the League in spite of imperfections. Responding to a prize essay contest announced in 1923, Roosevelt prepared an entry which advocated an international organization to replace the League. Less centralized than the existing body, the proposed association did provide a method of collective security but was less rigid than the Covenant.[6] Roosevelt's continued interest in world affairs and the challenge of maintaining peace is revealed by his deep concern over the foreign-policy planks of the Democratic platform in the 1928 election and his article published in *Foreign Affairs* that year. Temporizing between what seemed a proclivity toward greater American international involvement and the evident popularity of noninvolvement or at least the absence of commitment, Roosevelt sought to influence his party and at the same time avoid a position contrary to party or public sentiment. He did abandon his former big-navy stance to ridicule shipbuilding programs, but he urged "cooperation" with the League and seemed to support membership in the

6. Frank Freidel, *The Ordeal* (*Franklin D. Roosevelt,* Vol. II) (Boston, 1954), 127–29.

World Court. Though he was constant in his devotion to foreign policy, his avowed position on the issues was not always consistent. Whether from party considerations, domestic sentiments, changing circumstances, honest conviction, or a combination of these or other factors, Roosevelt dealt with the question but occasionally equivocated on the answers.

In the decade following the armistice, Roosevelt probably became even more convinced that in the realm of international relations, at least, idealism must be subordinated to realism. Compromise to satisfy domestic and foreign aspirations seemed axiomatic, with diplomacy the art of the possible under the guise of varying concepts of national interest or appealing abstractions. Yet Roosevelt opposed the popular Kellogg-Briand Pact for the "outlawry of war," contending that it lacked machinery for implementation and gave the false impression that the United States was assuming a leadership role in world affairs.[7] With his election to the governorship of New York, Roosevelt became immersed in the problems of the most populous state in the Union and the necessity to cope with the most severe depression in the nation's history. The priority of economic dislocation and unemployment continued with his accession to the presidency, although, as will be revealed later, he took initial steps to provide for greater American cooperation in resisting or deterring aggression and maintaining peace.

Contributing to Roosevelt's adoption of the unconditional surrender policy was his familiarity, as an avid if amateur student of history, with the fluctuations in war aims which had characterized American conflicts. The first such venture, the American Revolution, began as a limited war with a limited objective, namely, to secure a redress of "wrongs" from the mother country. In the "Declaration of Causes of Taking Up Arms," adopted July 6, 1775, the Representatives of the United Colonies of North America (the Continental Congress) enumerated their grievances, denounced the "cruel aggres-

7. *Ibid.,* 238; Franklin D. Roosevelt, "Our Foreign Policy: A Democratic View," *Foreign Affairs,* VI (1928), 573–86.

sion" begun at Lexington and Concord, gave assurances that "We mean not to dissolve that union which has so long and so happily subsisted between us, and which we wish to see restored," and concluded by imploring the "supreme and impartial Judge and Ruler of the Universe . . . to dispose our adversaries to reconciliation on reasonable terms. . . ." Within a year this same body formally renounced its modest objectives for the more extreme goal of independence. Thus during the course of hostilities the domestic rebellion was transformed into a war of national liberation for the thirteen colonies and eventually into a world conflict as the Americans escalated their military commitment and their aims. The struggle also marked the nation's first exposure to the complexities of coalition warfare, an experience not to be repeated for more than a hundred and fifty years.

The Quasi-War with France, when Congress by two successive acts in 1798 authorized the capture of French armed vessels, witnessed a diminution of war aims to the point where President John Adams's former Secretary of State, Timothy Pickering, caustically observed, "Instead of 'making peace on his own terms' he received the law from France." As a navy buff, Roosevelt was quite familiar with the humiliations suffered by the United States at the hands of the Barbary powers, where some of the treaties represented not compromise but capitulation. On a grander scale, the "peace of Christmas Eve" which concluded the War of 1812 achieved none of the declared or "hidden" objectives of the conflict. During the diplomatic negotiations, which began at Ghent relatively early in the war, the claims of each adversary gradually shifted from an insistence on extreme concessions to the virtual withdrawal of all demands and a settlement on the basis of the *status quo ante*. Moreover, on each side the modification of terms fluctuated with the course of hostilities in the Western Hemisphere and developments on the European scene, and the final treaty reflected the fact that neither the United States nor Great Britain had triumphed militarily.

In keeping with what was to become a virtual American tradition, another major war erupted a generation later. Although publicly President James K. Polk denied that the war with Mexico was designed for conquest, privately to his cabinet, as he put it, "I declared my purpose to be to acquire for the United States, California, New Mexico, and perhaps some others of the Northern Provinces of Mexico whenever a peace was made." [8] Disappointed though he may have been at not acquiring "some others of the Northern Provinces," the disparity between declared and actual war aims was apparent, and the failure to secure more territory was attributable to the recalcitrance of the Mexicans; the stubbornness of Polk's emissary, Nicholas Trist; and the congressional opposition to a continuation of the war. The degree of military commitment exceeded that contemplated by the President, who had anticipated a classical limited war with the military means circumscribed to be commensurate with the desired aims. Evidently the Mexicans felt that the stakes warranted a greater effort, for the northern campaign had to be supplemented by an invasion from the south and the capture of Mexico City before a treaty could be imposed. And for the first and only time a president was censured by the House of Representatives for his conduct of a war.

The Civil War provided Roosevelt with his favorite example of "unconditional surrender," which he inaccurately identified with Grant's terms to Lee at Appomattox.[9] While the nickname "Unconditional Surrender Grant" derived from the General's unequivocal terms at Fort Donelson, the war aims successively promulgated by President Abraham Lincoln did expand significantly. Throughout the conflict the President insisted that the southern states accept Federal authority, but after the Emancipation Proclamation he refused to permit dis-

8. Allan Nevins, ed., *Polk: The Diary of a President, 1845–1849* (London, 1929), 106.
9. Press conference, July 29, 1944, in Rosenman, *1944–45: The Threshold of Peace (Public Papers and Addresses of Franklin D. Roosevelt,* Vol. XIII) 209–10.

cussions unless the Confederacy accepted in advance "the restoration of the Union and the abandonment of slavery." By 1865 Lincoln had added another "indispensable" prerequisite, namely, "No cessation of hostilities short of an end of the war and the disbanding of all forces hostile to the government." All of the President's conditions were met with the complete military victory of the Union forces and the dissolution of the Confederate government. The escalation of demands may have stimulated southern resistance, but it probably also served to strengthen the President's hand, and he steadfastly refused to compromise.

As a young man at Groton, Roosevelt was caught up in the excitement that accompanied the Spanish-American War. Having read some of Mahan's books, he followed the course of battle with interest and even contemplated volunteering. Nor could he have avoided observing the widespread confusion over the aims of what Secretary of State John Hay later dubbed the "splendid little war." When President William McKinley asked Congress for authority to bring an end to the conflict in Cuba he received a mandate to give the island its freedom. With each battle success, the American demands accelerated to the point where the nation acquired an overseas empire. The influence of these events on a sixteen-year-old youth schooled in Mahan and observing the exploits of his elder cousin must have been considerable.

Roosevelt's proclivity for American participation in World War I has been mentioned, although it is not certain that he shared many of Wilson's war aims. Actually, Wilson was not always clear in defining his goals, which appeared to change as the American military commitment intensified. German resumption of unrestricted submarine warfare may have provoked Wilson's war message, but his declared objective embraced not only an observance of the rights of neutral nations but the mission of making the world safe for democracy. Subsequent public expositions of war aims, epitomized by the popular Fourteen Points, found Wilson calling for an entire new world order designed to reduce frictions that might lead to war and provide a mechanism for the enforcement of collective security. But the President found himself enmeshed in the coils not only of coalition warfare but of coalition diplomacy as well. His technical distinction which labeled the United States an "associated" rather than an "allied" power was artificial in regard to the waging of the war and the making of the peace, and those nations that had borne the brunt of the Central Powers' military onslaught were not in the mood to accept Wilson's "noble" or "idealistic" terms when the victors met at Versailles.

Disagreement arose in part over the correlation of the amount of sacrifice with the "voice" that each nation should have in determining the nature of the settlement. It also involved age-old aspirations that could be achieved only at the expense of Wilson's principles. To aggravate the dissension, secret treaties were revealed which pledged specific distributions of the spoils in a manner inconsistent with the President's formulations. The entire episode constituted a veritable case study in the problems involved in making a peace, especially a coalition peace, and the compromises necessitated by conflicting ambitions could have served as an object lesson to any American statesman who had the temerity to contemplate political involvement in Old World affairs.

The disparate objectives of the various belligerents, the diffusion of war and peace aims, and the unsatisfactory outcome of Wilson's valiant efforts made an indelible impression on the ambitious young Assistant Secretary of the Navy. He saw the President's idealistic proposals ridiculed in the press and the Congress; modified, at times beyond recognition, by leaders of the nations he had helped save; and defeated by a recalcitrant Senate that demanded compromises he would not accept. In the years that followed Roosevelt's unsuccessful bid for the vice presidency and his tragic affliction with infantile paralysis, he availed himself of the opportunity to observe events throughout the world and contemplate the shortcomings of the solution proscribed at Versailles. Among the many questions he deliberated were the following: (1) Did Wilson, by delegating authority for the military strategy of the war, abrogate his Constitutional responsibility as Commander in Chief and weaken his influence in determining the provisions of the peace? (2) Were the Allied and Associated Powers "surprised into peace," without adequate preparation or even discussion among themselves on war aims? (3) To what extent should details of the final settlement be made public, and at what point should they be negotiated among members of a coalition? (4) Should an armistice be concluded that incorporated conditions which inhibited the actions of the victors or made them vulnerable to the accusation of having violated an agreement? (5) At what time and under what circumstances should a final peace conference be held? (6) In what way should the President become involved in negotiations, either directly or through subordinates? (7) What was the appropriate role for members of Congress and military leaders in the deliberations related to political matters, either concerning the waging of the war or the conclusion of a peace? While Roosevelt may not have anticipated the opportunity to avoid a repetition of Wilson's mistakes, his own experience, interests, and aspirations made inevitable his unflagging concern with these questions. His conclusions were to alter the course of human events.

2

The President and International Anarchy

THE PRESIDENTIAL CAMPAIGN of 1932 gave little indication of new or startling departures in the realm of foreign policy, largely because of the urgency of the domestic crisis. But as president-elect, Roosevelt did endorse the Hoover-Stimson Doctrine, which denied recognition of territory acquired by the use of force—a policy invoked against Japan when her troops invaded Manchuria in 1931; and he announced his support for a pending bill that would allow the president to embargo the export of arms to a nation which he designated an aggressor.[1] Although this legislation never received congressional approval, Roosevelt as president continued his efforts to provide for greater American collaboration in the direction of world affairs. Committed by his predecessor to participation in the World Disarmament Conference at Geneva, Roosevelt authorized his chief delegate, Norman Davis, to offer concessions far exceeding those contemplated by the three previous Republican occupants of the White House. Davis proposed a nonaggression pact committing nations to refrain from sending troops beyond their own borders

1. Bernard Sternsher, "The Stimson Doctrine: F.D.R. *versus* Moley and Tugwell," *Pacific Historical Review,* XXXI (1962), 281–89; Elton Atwater, *American Regulation of Arms Exports* (Washington, 1941), 188–92, Robert A. Divine, "Franklin D. Roosevelt and Collective Security, 1933," *Mississippi Valley Historical Review,* XLVIII (1961), 42–59.

and offered to consult with other nations in the event of a threat
to the peace. He urged adoption of the international supervision of armaments and pledged the United States to avoid
interference with sanctions imposed on an aggressor by the
League, provided the Washington government concurred in the
designation. Marking a drastic departure from previous American proposals to encourage a reduction of armaments and
participate in efforts for collective security, these bold overtures were lost as the conference failed over disagreement on
other issues.

For several years following this initial venture the President
refrained from further attempts to commit the nation to cooperative action for the preservation of peace or resistance to
aggression. Whether he was deterred from following an "interventionist" line by the inability of the European nations to
implement disarmament, by domestic opposition, or by a con-
centration on the pressing problems at home is not clear. In
the meantime his rejection of the gold-standard position taken
by the European governments at the London Economic Conference in 1933 gave evidence of a nationalist tendency, at least
in regard to monetary policy, and some interpreted his stance
as a reassertion of United States isolationism. Latin American
relations continued to follow that of the Good Neighbor, with
the final withdrawal of troops from Haiti and the abrogation
of the Platt Amendment, which had permitted intervention in
the internal affairs of Cuba.

The investigation of the Senate committee under Gerald
Nye in 1934–35 on munitions profiteering during World War I,
and an outcry against "merchants of death" coincided with the
outbreak of the Italo-Ethiopian conflict in 1935 and helped
induce Congress to pass neutrality legislation designed to keep
the country out of war. Prohibiting the sale of weapons to the
belligerents when the president should determine that a state
of war existed, the bill was signed by Roosevelt in spite of
his desire for authority to impose a "discretionary embargo"

against the aggressor nation.[2] Under the circumstances, the administration did urge a "moral embargo" against the export of oil, which was of greatest value to the Italian war machine, but otherwise was incapable of supporting the moderate economic sanctions imposed by the League against the "invader." Roosevelt, searching for some means of exerting American influence to preserve peace, followed the lead of Great Britain and France in trying to "insulate" the Spanish Civil War, which erupted in 1936, and he supported legislation to prohibit arms shipments to both sides. When the Sino-Japanese conflict resumed in July 1937, Roosevelt apparently decided it was time to assume the initiative. Mussolini had successfully defied the League in Ethiopia, the Spanish situation had degenerated into a "proxy war" between fascism and communism, and the Far East again was ablaze. The latter offered a more immediate direct threat to American interests, but the international anarchy that prevailed seemed likely to engulf the Western Hemisphere if not controlled.

The President selected Chicago, the center of alleged midwestern isolationism, as the location for his appeal. Speaking on October 5, 1937, Roosevelt called attention to the spread of the "epidemic of world lawlessness," described war as a "contagion," and asked for a "quarantine" of aggressors by peace-loving nations. What specific steps the President had in mind were not revealed, and he may have been dissuaded from following up his suggestion by a vehement if minority outcry against American participation in any attempt at collective security. Nevertheless, the State Department a day later denounced the Japanese activity in China as a violation of the Nine-Power Treaty of 1922 and the Kellogg-Briand Pact, and endorsed a report condemning Japan approved by the Assembly of the League of Nations.

Still hoping to resolve the Sino-Japanese conflict, Roosevelt

2. For an account of neutrality legislation, see Robert A. Divine, *The Illusion of Neutrality* (Chicago, 1962).

sent representatives to a meeting at Brussels in November
1937. Called under the provisions of the Nine-Power Treaty
but boycotted by Japan, the conference failed to produce any
substantive solution. Contributing to the failure may have been
a directive to the American delegation prohibiting even a discussion of economic sanctions, much less their application.
Roosevelt continued to avoid commitments that might involve
the nation in activities anathema to significant segments of
the press, the public, and the Congress. His response, however, was not confined solely to pronouncements and exhortations. The President refused to invoke the Neutrality Act in the
Far Eastern conflict, ostensibly because neither Japan nor
China admitted that a state of war existed. Conventionally
interpreted as a move to continue the supply of aid to China,
the victim of aggression, Roosevelt's motive evidently included
a reluctance to offend Japan, interfere with a lucrative trade,
or spur further military ventures.

Presidential caution in the conduct of foreign affairs was
again revealed by the reaction to the unprovoked Japanese
attack on the American gunboat *Panay* and three merchant
tankers in the Yangtze River in December 1937. Roosevelt
may have been disconcerted by the immediate Japanese apol-
ogy and offer to make reparations, and he must have been
impressed by the lack of public indignation at what appeared
to be the most blatant of atrocities. Perhaps acceding to an
evidently widespread feeling that any action tending to provoke war should be avoided, the President confined his response to a stiff diplomatic note hastily accepted by the
Japanese, who agreed to comply with the stated demands.
Roosevelt also may have been prevented from taking more
positive steps to indicate displeasure by his realization that the
American navy was not prepared to support unilaterally any
more drastic action that might be contemplated against Japan.
The fleet was not maintained at war complement in personnel,
and logistically it was not capable of operations in the western
Pacific against a formidable Japanese navy which enjoyed the

proximity of bases.

The incident did have its repercussions, for it probably brought Roosevelt to a greater awareness of the seriousness of the threat to American interests posed by the unbridled military activity of the Axis Powers. In January 1938, the month following the *Panay* incident, the President embarked on two courses of action. First, in a special message to Congress he requested a sizeable increase in naval appropriations to expand and develop the fleet; second, he made secret overtures to Great Britain for joint efforts to restrain aggression and recodify rules of international behavior. The congressional response to the request for naval rearmament was generally favorable, but Prime Minister Neville Chamberlain rejected the President's appeal in the hope that another tack would prove more rewarding. The apogee of "appeasement" was reached at Munich in October 1938, when it appeared that the appetites of the European dictators were satisfied. Roosevelt seemed to share with many others a feeling of relief that war had been avoided and prospects for peace appeared brighter, an illusion soon dispelled when Germany annexed the remainder of Czechoslovakia in the spring of 1939. Both Great Britain and France hastily concluded defense pacts with Poland, which gave every indication of being the next victim of Hitler's ambition, and rearmament accelerated as the nations girded themselves for the anticipated crisis.

The President was not completely taken in by the Munich settlement, and he continued to alert the country to the dangers threatening American security. Addressing Congress on January 4, 1939, he warned that the United States could not ignore events in other parts of the world or avoid measures to discourage aggression. Urging that the nation's defenses be strengthened, he noted, "There are many methods short of war, but stronger and more effective than mere words, of bringing home to aggressor governments the aggregate sentiments of our own people." Privately he voiced the opinion that there would have been no "surrender" at Munich if the British

Government had possessed an air force of five thousand planes, and in January 1939 he told the Senate Foreign Relations Committee that America's first line of defense in the Atlantic was on the Rhine, with that extreme part of the perimeter being protected by the Western opponents of Hitler's Germany. As the European situation worsened in the spring of that year, Roosevelt sought to implement his "methods short of war" by securing a change in existing neutrality legislation to permit a "cash and carry" sale of munitions to belligerents. Hoping to discourage Hitler from further aggression by the prospect of American industrial production being available to the powers controlling the sea lanes as in World War I, the President waged a losing battle with a Congress determined to avoid a repetition of what some believed was responsible for drawing the nation into that earlier conflict.

Roosevelt's grand strategy was nationally oriented but worldwide in scope. Of primary strategic concern were the safety and security of the United States, its possessions in the Pacific and the Caribbean, the entire Western Hemisphere, and American interests abroad. The global nature of the defense perimeter demanded the prevention or containment of hostilities in the Far East and in Europe to prevent domination of either area by an unfriendly power or combination of powers which could jeopardize America's vital interests. The balance in Asia was being upset by the militancy of Japan, and Hitler's unilateral revisions of the Treaty of Versailles revealed a similar development in Europe. Aware that multilateral and unilateral efforts to maintain the *status quo* had failed, the President sought for more positive ways to influence events. In so doing he was faced not only with the problem of what should be done but with the exasperating limitations of what could be done. His most immediate challenge was at home, for he had to convince his own countrymen of their crucial stake in developments geographically remote from the national frontiers. In trying to change what amounted to a deeply ingrained national concensus based on emotional and rational aversions to foreign "embroilments" and foreign wars, the President was compelled to employ his considerable forensic talents, his persuasive arts, his educational and leadership abilities, his manipulative genius, and what some would regard as his Machiavellian inclinations. The extent to which Roosevelt was successful is debatable, for he had to tread warily to avoid a vigorous domestic rejection of his program. If he went too far or too fast he might find himself and his concept repudiated, with, from his point of view, disastrous consequences for the United States and the world.

The President was not conducting foreign policy in a vacuum, either internally or externally. While the final important decisions were his, he was subjected to information and advice, solicited and unsolicited, from a variety of sources. To understand the behavior and intentions of other nations he relied heavily on the State Department, which gathered reports from duly accredited representatives abroad. Bypassing this normal channel were certain emissaries in key posts who, because of friendship or close political affiliation, occasionally communicated directly with the President. In this category were Ambassadors Joseph C. Grew in Tokyo, William C. Bullitt in Moscow and later Paris, and Joseph P. Kennedy in London. The army and naval attachés at the various embassies provided data on developments in the armed forces, and this information was passed to the White House through the departments of War and Navy. As the international scene darkened in the later 1930s, the President began to rely more heavily on the Chief of Staff of the army and the Chief of Naval Operations, for he insisted that in his role as Commander in Chief he must deal directly with the professional heads of the services without the intercession of the civilian secretaries. Military planning was coordinated by the Joint Army and Navy Board, established in 1903, but in April 1938 the President, at the urging of Secretary of State Hull, created a standing Liaison Committee of the State, War, and Navy departments. Designed to coordinate the planning and implementation of diplomatic and military policy, this group was composed of the Under Secretary of State, the army Chief of Staff, and the Chief of Naval Operations.

On the domestic front the Congress formed one of the most formidable obstacles to the President's attempt to move the nation toward a more "interventionist" position. Chairing the powerful Senate Foreign Relations Committee from 1933 until his death in 1940 was Senator Key Pittman of Nevada, who followed a middle-of-the-road course in regard to American involvement abroad. With outspoken colleagues on every side of the issue in both houses, Pittman played a significant role in avoiding a complete break in direction between the legislative and executive branches of the government. At the same time he reflected a widespread attitude shared by many members of Congress and a large portion of the public which feared that the President was intent on committing the nation to actions leading to war. Roosevelt, dependent on congressional support to implement certain crucial policies, could not risk a direct confrontation that would imperil his entire program.[3]

The administration continued to make known its displeasure over the antics of the dictators, apply "moral" force by public reprimand to discourage aggression, and add its weight to the cause of peace. When Germany annexed the remainder of Czechoslovakia, Hull denounced the move, and Roosevelt used the occasion of an address to the Pan American Union to castigate the predators. In April the President appealed personally to Hitler and Mussolini, asking that they assure their neighbors that territorial boundaries were inviolate; but his only reply came in a sarcastic diatribe by the Führer before the Reichstag, ridiculing the notion that any country bordering Germany was in the least concerned. At the end of Caribbean fleet maneuvers in the spring of 1939, when major units were scheduled to visit the World's Fair in New York, the

---

3. Wayne S. Cole, "Senator Key Pittman and American Neutrality Policies, 1933–1940," *The Mississippi Valley Historical Review*, XLVI (March 1960), 644–62.

President abruptly ordered their return to the Pacific coast. Britain, finding it necessary to concentrate her efforts on the deteriorating European scene, could no longer afford to maintain pressure on Japan, and the United States prepared to assume a greater responsibility in the Far East. Yet all of the President's efforts to influence the course of events proved unavailing, and the invasion of Poland on September 1, 1939, heralded the beginning of another and more devastating world war. This final breakdown of collective security a mere twenty years after the conclusion of a massive "war to end all wars" marked the culmination of the most vigorous concerted endeavors to preserve peace in the annals of man. The bold League of Nations, the regional pacts such as those of Locarno, the bilateral nonaggression treaties, and the defensive military alliances all had failed to prevent the outbreak of another world holocaust. As Alfred North Whitehead has observed, "The folly of intelligent people, clear-headed and narrow visioned, has precipitated many catastrophes."

Among the factors contributing to the outbreak of the Second World War were the shortcomings of the armistice and the Treaty of Versailles, America's failure to join the League, a reluctance on the part of the major powers to use force or the threat of force at crucial times, inadequate application of sanctions, inconsistent cooperation between Britain and France, the impact of the economic depression, and the unbridled ambitions of predatory nations. These "causes," and others more subtle if not less potentially explosive, were discernible to the President, and his perception of the origins of the war was directly related to the way he thought the war should end and the steps that he thought should be taken to prevent a recurrence.

The President responded to the onset of European hostilities by a formal declaration of neutrality, although, unlike Wilson, he did not ask that people be neutral in thought, and he resumed his earlier attempt to revise the existing neutrality act to permit the sale of munitions to belligerents. Declaring a limited emergency, he summoned Congress to a special session and was successful in securing a repeal of the arms embargo to permit "cash and carry" sales. While a lull in fighting followed Poland's defeat and Anglo-French forces continued to face temporarily sated Germany, Roosevelt in the early spring of 1940 sent Under Secretary of State Sumner Welles to Europe as his special emissary. Announced as a fact-finding trip, Welles's actual mission was to talk with the heads of state in England, France, Germany, and Italy about "the present possibility of the establishment in Europe of a stable and lasting peace." The Nazi leaders wanted predominance in Central Europe, special economic privileges with the nations of eastern and southeastern Europe, military security on Germany's frontiers, the return of colonies "stolen" at Versailles, and an end to the determination by England and France to "destroy Germany." The British Prime Minister, Neville Chamberlain, denied that Britain had designs on the German people or nation, but he emphatically declared that peace with the Nazi Government which was bent on military conquest was impossible. Winston Churchill, then First Lord of the Admiralty, was more explicit. There must be a "complete defeat" of Germany, National Socialism must be destroyed, provision had to be made for controlling German aspirations, and Austria, Poland, and Czechoslovakia must be re-established. Russia, he felt, "offered no real menace and no real problem."

In his report to the President, Welles revealed that each side was insistent on terms palpably unacceptable to the other, and that it was fruitless for the United States to pursue the matter.[4] To further complicate the situation, the Soviet Union had invaded Finland after having shared in the partition of Poland, and sympathies became even more divided as the

---

4. Material on the Welles mission may be found in U.S. State Department, *Foreign Relations of the United States, Diplomatic Papers, 1940*, I (Washington, 1959), 1–117. For German war aims, see *ibid.*, 38–53; for British, *ibid.*, 76–84. This series hereafter will be cited as *FR*, followed by year and volume number.

Anglo-French allies pondered a response to this latest aggression.

The spring of 1940 brought an end to uncertainty. Hitler broke the stalemate with an attack on Norway and the occupation of Denmark, and while the Allies were reeling from their ineffectual attempts to counter these moves, the unpredictable Führer struck at Belgium, Holland, and France. When it soon became apparent that the German military machine could not be stopped, frantic appeals were made to Washington for American intervention. The President, helpless in the antiwar attitude gripping the country, could respond only with heartening words encouraging continued resistance and promising to furnish weapons.[5] With the signing of the armistice between Germany and France in June 1940, only England remained as Germany's foe, an England battered and bloody from a rout that culminated in the evacuation of the British, French, and Belgian armies at Dunkirk. No longer was Hitler's defeat the primary concern, for of higher priority was the preservation of the final bastion standing between the Axis tide and the Western Hemisphere.

A more severe blow to the President's hopes can scarcely be imagined. He had counted heavily on the ability of the Anglo-French combination to contain Hitler and eventually prevail with moral and material aid from the United States. Now the first line of American defense, those buffer states on the continent of Europe, was gone, and only militarily threadbare Britain remained. The possibility that the partners in the rape of Poland, Germany and Russia, would fall out seemed remote, and the imperative of Britain's survival was immediate. Meanwhile the President was engaged in a campaign for re-election in which each candidate stressed the question that was uppermost in the minds of the electorate: whether the nation would again be involved in war.

5. The few "interventionist" groups were relatively ineffectual. See Mark Lincoln Chadwin, *The Warhawks: American Interventionists before Pearl Harbor* (New York, 1970).

Both Roosevelt and his Republican opponent, Wendell Willkie, pledged a dedication to peace, and each insisted that his policies were designed to keep America out of war. But the President gave assurances that American boys were not going to fight in a "foreign war," and he rejected suggestions that he should add the qualifying phrase "except in case of attack" by irritably remarking that in that event it would not be a foreign war. In spite of a widespread skepticism over electioneering promises, the President may have believed sincerely that any conflict resulting from a direct threat to the safety and security of the United States, regardless whether it was an attack, would not be in the category of a foreign war. His subsequent action would so indicate, as would his general strategic approach to world affairs and their impact, immediate or future, on American interests.

During the campaign Roosevelt's firm resolve to help Britain survive was revealed when he responded to an urgent appeal by providing fifty World War I destroyers in exchange for rights to certain bases in the Western Hemisphere. Beleaguered England relied for its very existence on supplies from its dependencies and the United States, and German raiders threatened to sever the British life lines. The President finally decided to effect the transfer by executive order rather than follow the time-consuming and politically explosive legislative route. Involved in the action were the propriety of a professed neutral furnishing warships to a belligerent, and the Constitutional authority of the president to dispose of the vessels. Equally disturbing to some critics was the further commitment to the British cause, but Willkie endorsed the exchange and denounced only the method which ignored Congress.[6] After his re-election, Roosevelt sought to relieve Britain's economic plight and eliminate what he referred to as the "silly old dollar sign" by sponsoring the Lend-Lease Bill,

6. See *FR, 1940,* III, 49–77; and Philip Goodhart, *Fifty Ships that Saved the World: The Foundation of the Anglo-American Alliance* (Garden City, N.Y., 1965).

which finally became law in the spring of 1941. Designed to overcome the stigma attached to the unpaid loans of the First World War, this legislation allowed the President to provide war materiel to victims of aggression.[7] The United States formally had assumed its role as the arsenal of democracy.

The debate over Lend-Lease again brought to the fore most of the arguments that had accompanied every attempt by the President to strengthen his hand against the dictators. Both sides, with rare exceptions, allegedly were motivated by a desire to keep America out of war, but they differed on the method. The President's supporters shared his contention that aid to the aggressors' victims would save America from eventual involvement; his opponents contended that it would serve to accelerate participation. The numerous peace groups were similarly divided as the world situation rapidly deteriorated, and the obscure average citizen found himself overwhelmed by the barrage of rhetoric and invective which seemed to cloud rather than clarify the options available to America.[8]

Among the options available to the President were those he could exercise in his capacity as Commander in Chief of the army and navy. After annual fleet maneuvers in early 1940, he ordered the ships to remain in Hawaii rather than return to their regular bases in California. Designed to intimidate the Japanese and discourage further aggressive moves, this deterrent albeit provocative action was followed by an order calling up naval reservists and raising the peacetime allowance of personnel aboard ship to the full wartime complement. The "security zone" patrol around the Americas which had been established in 1939 was reinforced, in May 1941 major units of the Pacific fleet were transferred to the Atlantic to provide support for the British navy, and by fall

7. See Warren F. Kimball, *The Most Unsordid Act: Lend-Lease, 1939–1941* (Baltimore, 1969).
8. For views of different groups, see Manfred Jonas, *Isolationism in America, 1935–1941* (Ithaca, N.Y., 1966); and Mark Lincoln Chadwin, *The Warhawks: American Interventionists before Pearl Harbor* (New York, 1970).

of 1941 American warships were engaged in the escort of convoys and an unofficial shooting war with German submarines.[9] Meanwhile, Roosevelt's speeches became increasingly belligerent as he sought to provide more assistance to Britain and Hitler's latest victim, the Soviet Union. The President first announced his views on the postwar world in an address to Congress on January 6, 1941, in which he advocated four universal human freedoms: freedom of speech, freedom of worship, freedom from want, and freedom from fear. A further elaboration of these ideals appeared in a joint declaration following his momentous conference with Churchill near Argentia, Newfoundland, in August 1941. This document, later known as the Atlantic Charter, contained eight principles which were to prevail "after the final destruction of the Nazi tyranny." The full implications of the dramatic meeting were not clear at the time, although in England the government encouraged the impression that the two leaders had formed a virtual alliance binding America to partnership in the war against Germany. Obviously, the President had no Constitutional authority to make such an agreement, and the wording of the eight points warranted no such interpretation. On the other hand, the tenor of the declaration was unmistakable, and Roosevelt had pledged continued support in the struggle. He did reiterate his previous request that the British government not make any secret agreements with its allies without the knowledge or consent of the United States, probably wanting to avoid Wilson's embarrassing experience and ensure full participation in postwar planning.[10] The Prime Minister tried in vain to persuade the President to warn Japan

9. An especially perceptive study is Robert J. Quinlan, "The United States Fleet: Diplomacy, Strategy and the Allocation of Ships (1940–1941)," in Harold Stein, ed., *American Civil-Military Decisions: A Book of Case Studies* (Birmingham, Ala., 1963), 153–98.

10. As early as July 14, 1941, Roosevelt in a message to Churchill asked that the British government not make secret commitments with its allies without the knowledge or consent of the United States. *FR, 1941,* I, 342.

that an attack on British or Dutch territory would provoke American retaliation, but the meeting did constitute a propaganda victory which Churchill exploited to the full in despair-ridden England.[11]

Negotiations between Washington and Tokyo had reached their most critical stage with the recent freezing of Japanese assets in the United States and the imposition of an embargo on the export of oil to Japan, an action followed by Britain and the Netherlands. Roosevelt had begun to apply economic sanctions against Japan in 1938 with a "moral" embargo discouraging the export of aircraft parts. Two days after the signing of the Craigie-Arita agreement on July 24, 1939, by which Britain acknowledged Japan's primary interests in China, the United States gave six months' notice of termination of the 1911 commercial treaty with Japan. Subsequent restrictions on the export of various strategic commodities and the retention of the American fleet at Hawaii evoked further protests from Tokyo and evasive responses from Washington. But the combination of economic sanctions and intimidating naval dispositions indicated that the United States was determined to thwart Japanese ambitions in the Far East, and the protracted conversations between representatives of the two governments gave little promise of a reconciliation. The Japanese government intended to establish a new order in the Far East, which it labeled the Greater East Asia Co-Prosperity Sphere. Embracing China, Southeast Asia, and later the islands of the southwest Pacific, this ambitious plan was designed to exploit the natural and human resources of these areas.

Why, it may be asked, was the President applying increased pressure on the Japanese when the situation in Europe was so desperate? Certainly he was concerned over the fate of China and the threat to American interests in Asia. But he had refrained from using more coercive measures to induce Japan

11. A full account of the epochal meeting is contained in Theodore A. Wilson, *The First Summit: Roosevelt and Churchill at Placentia Bay 1941* (Boston, 1969).

to mend its ways until after the breakdown of the Munich agreement. As Hitler continued to upset the European equilibrium and Britain became more involved attempting to contain him, Roosevelt intensified the pressure on Japan by an acceleration of economic sanctions and more vigorous diplomatic negotiation. He responded to each new Japanese initiative, such as the move into French Indochina after the fall of France, by the institution of a new embargo on vital materials and eventually the final act in July 1941 of freezing assets and prohibiting the export of oil. Why this seeming diversion of effort when the European scene was so critical and American involvement there was barely short of overt war?

One plausible explanation, which this writer accepts, is that the President was trying to prevent Japan from doing anything that would directly affect the course of the war in Europe. Japan had taken advantage of Hitler's successes to advance her own ambitions, which, it appeared, would best be served either by a southward thrust into British and Dutch holdings or by an assault on the Soviet Union to aid Germany and eliminate Russia as a power in the Far East. The choice between the rich resources of the East Indies and Southeast Asia versus a share in the destruction of a long-time rival for domination in China was debated at length in Tokyo and finally resolved in favor of the former. Roosevelt, aware of both possibilities, realized the dire implications of either move for the European struggle. The southern strike would provide Japan with badly needed oil for her military and industrial machine, deprive England of her Pacific empire, and compel her to sue for an armistice. The alternative could be equally disastrous by ensuring the capitulation of the Soviet Union and establishing Hitler's absolute domination of the European continent. Fundamental to the President's strategy was the continuance of Chinese resistance, for its collapse would free Japanese troops to carry out either or possibly both of the contemplated operations with a catastrophic effect on the European conflict. Roosevelt's world strategy was primarily European oriented, and his actions in the Far East were designed to prevent Japan from aiding Hitler in any decisive manner.

So as the President continued to support the British and Russian war effort with every means at his disposal, his steadily increasing pressure on Japan convinced the Tokyo government that, barring a last-minute change in Washington's policy, war was unavoidable. When the minimal concessions were not forthcoming, the Japanese task force struck the American fleet at Pearl Harbor to immobilize naval opposition to the projected military operations in the southwest Pacific. Anticipating American intervention if British and Dutch possessions were invaded, the Japanese authorities chose to surprise the fleet at anchor rather than wait for a "classic" naval engagement in the western Pacific.[12]

12. The Japanese rationale for the "Hawaii Operation" is presented in Raymond G. O'Connor, ed., *The Japanese Navy in World War II* (Annapolis, Md., 1969), 2–27.

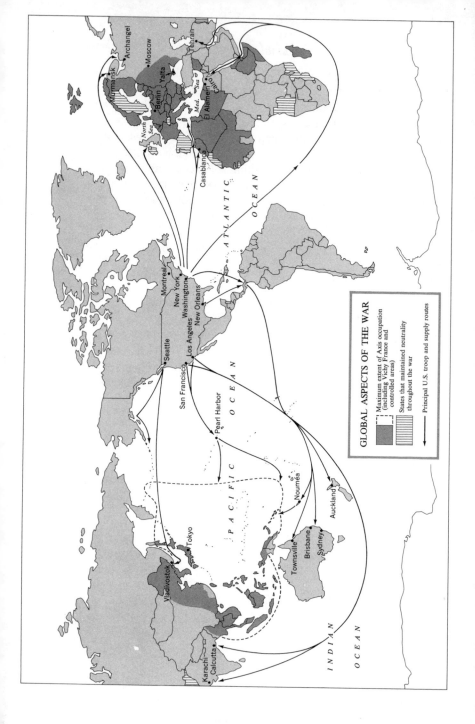

GLOBAL ASPECTS OF THE WAR

Maximum extent of Axis occupation (including Vichy France and controlled areas)

States that maintained neutrality throughout the war

Principal U.S. troop and supply routes

Archangel · Moscow · Tehran · Murmansk Berlin · Yalta · El Alamein · Cairo · Casablanca · *North Sea · Med. Sea*

Montreal · New York · Washington · New Orleans · Seattle · San Francisco · Los Angeles · Pearl Harbor

Vladivostok · Tokyo · Nouméa · Auckland · Townsville · Brisbane · Sydney · Karachi · Calcutta

ATLANTIC OCEAN · PACIFIC OCEAN · INDIAN OCEAN

3

The Politics of Military Strategy

WHEN WITHIN A FEW DAYS both Germany and Italy declared war on the United States, the stage was set for an implementation of the Anglo-American broad strategy that had been agreed to earlier. Conversations and formal meetings between the military staffs of the two nations, which had been held on an irregular basis for some time, had resulted in the decision that a "Germany first" policy would be followed in the event of a two-ocean war. With the Japanese advance unchecked in the western Pacific, the desperate plight of the forces in the Philippines, and the deteriorating situation in China, the European-oriented strategy was viewed by some as an aberration. Although a public opinion poll taken soon after the attack on Pearl Harbor revealed that over sixty percent of the respondents favored a "Japan first" policy, there was no inclination by the President to change the previously established plan. The major source of contention between the two staffs, a dispute which had begun in earlier discussions and was to jeopardize the very continuance of the alliance, was over the method by which the defeat of the arch-enemy Hitler should be accomplished. Behind these opposing viewpoints were deep-seated convictions, with historical, ideological, and rational bases. The implications of these divergent strategies transcended the "purely military" dimensions of the war, for the manner in which the war was waged could scarcely fail to affect the conditions of the peace.

Whether the British or the American approach best served the common war aims must, of necessity, constitute a large part of this story. Nations ordinarily resort to armed conflict not for the sake of combat itself but in order to promote particular national interests. Therefore, the war should be conducted in a way that provides the greatest opportunity to achieve the desired objectives. Ideally, the military strategy should be so designed that it will bring about conditions best suited to the establishment of the eventual peace.

Essentially, the British authorities envisioned an indirect or peripheral strategy which would nibble away at the edges of the German-Italian stronghold and wear it down by a process of attrition. Heavy bombing raids and naval blockade would disrupt the economy, weaken the warmaking potential, and destroy enemy morale. Underground resistance movements in occupied countries and even in Germany itself would rise against the oppressors, who then would find themselves unable to offer more than a token defense against the liberating forces of the Allies. The huge bloody campaigns of the First World War were to be avoided on the Western front at least.[1]

In contrast, the American planners conceived of a "direct" approach which sought an engagement with the main body of the enemy troops as quickly as possible in order to bring the conflict to an end. Any diversion of effort and resources which might delay the final blow was vigorously opposed by the American military leaders, who advocated a "second front" cross-channel invasion by 1943 at the latest. The dispute is especially relevant because it raged throughout much of the war, and the various postponements of the invasion had a significant effect on Allied harmony and the postwar situation.

Immersed in military planning, the President, while not averse to the promulgation of general principles regarding the postwar world, persistently refused to deal with specifics.

1. For a sustained defense of the "indirect approach," see B. H. Liddell Hart, *Strategy* (New York, 1954).

Shortly before the attack on Pearl Harbor, when the British were discussing a possible treaty with the Soviet Union, Secretary of State Cordell Hull cautioned London against any agreement on boundaries or territorial adjustments. When the United States became a formal member of the coalition against some or all of the Axis Powers, the President personally interceded to ensure the proper wording of the document to be known as the Declaration of the United Nations. Signed on January 1, 1942, the signatories subscribed to the principles of the Atlantic Charter,[2] affirmed that "complete victory over their enemies is essential," and pledged to "cooperate with the Governments signatory hereto and not to make a separate armistice or peace with the enemies." Roosevelt, not sure of his authority to make the latter commitment, asked Hull for an opinion. The Secretary forwarded to the President a memorandum prepared by the Department's legal adviser, Green H. Hackworth, which held that "While Congress has authority under the Constitution to declare war, once it is declared it is for the President to determine when peace may be concluded. He may conclude an armistice or negotiate a treaty of peace, or both. The armistice is wholly a function of the President but a treaty of peace requires senatorial approval." This authority stemmed, the memorandum concluded, from "his responsibility as Commander in Chief and his broad powers in the conduct of foreign relations."[3]

Just what might constitute "complete victory" was not explained, but the Allies were bound by a formal document to avoid a "separate armistice or peace." The circumstances under which fighting might cease were sufficiently clear for public consumption, the details of a settlement with the enemy were not stated, but a joint approach to the termination of hostilities was explicit. War aims were defined in terms general enough to secure the endorsement of all signatory governments and their cooperation in the formidable task ahead. For

2. See Appendix A.
3. *FR, 1942,* I, 9–12.

those nations not at war with Japan, including the Soviet Union, Article One stipulated, "Each Government pledges itself to employ its full resources, military or economic, against those members of the Tripartite Pact and its adherents *with which such government is at war.*" A press statement prepared by the Department of State referred to the declaration as an "alliance." Implying a treaty arrangement, this word was deleted by order of the Secretary prior to release.[4] Despite the technicality, however, this agreement did constitute the basis for the "grand alliance" that brought defeat to the enemy.

The President, carefully phrasing this document, was continuing a purposely vague definition of war aims. In his address to Congress after the Pearl Harbor attack, he gave assurances of "absolute victory." And while the congressional resolutions simply authorized the President "to bring the conflict to a successful termination," on December 9 he declared, "I repeat that the United States can accept no result save victory, final and complete." Two days later he forecast "a world victory of the forces of justice and of righteousness over the forces of savagery and of barbarism," and the term "total victory" appeared in his annual messages of January 6, 1942, and January 6, 1945. Roosevelt's public utterances during the war are studded with the word "victory," usually employed in the military sense, occasionally pertaining to the peace, and at times ambiguously embracing both.[5]

The emotional appeal of this laudable exhortation was undeniable, especially when invoked in a virtual crusade against the "evil," "diabolical," "aggressive" Axis nations. Not only did it provide a convenient slogan and unobjectionable goal around which all Americans could rally, but it avoided any position which could foment internal dissension that might interfere with the prosecution of the war. Nor were the

---

4. *Ibid.,* 29.

5. E.g., "Victory in this war is the first and greatest goal before us. Victory in the peace is the next." Address on the State of the Union, January 7, 1943. Rosenman, ed., *1943: The Tide Turns,* 32.

Allied governments able to quarrel with this commendable if equivocal objective. But aside from the general principles enumerated in the Atlantic Charter and the Declaration of the United Nations, the President carefully refrained from announcing or discussing more specific war aims in public; nor, apparently, was he anxious to resolve them in private.

What the President wanted in detail was not evident, but what he did *not* want is abundantly clear, namely, discord among the members of the coalition. Victory comprises many ingredients, but the most essential is military success. Without it none of the other components could be realized. And the most likely source of dissension among the Allies was not the question of the way the war should be fought, important and potentially lethal as this could be. More disruptive of unity in pursuing the common objective of defeating the enemy was a controversy over war aims. Roosevelt had participated in the lengthy negotiations that preceded agreement with Great Britain on the provisions of the Atlantic Charter, which had proved sufficiently ambiguous to gain endorsement by the signatories of the Declaration of the United Nations. Any attempt to elaborate on these principles was bound to raise issues over which the Allies would be divided, with disastrous consequences for the military effort. The substantive questions would surface occasionally, and they would have to be dealt with eventually, but delay was imperative to prevent a diversion from the massive task that lay ahead in halting, throwing back, and finally defeating the enemy.

So the first priority was providing for the prosecution of the war, and the conference in Washington during December–January 1941–42 found Roosevelt, Churchill, and their staffs concentrating on this formidable project. But the President did not ignore the long-range purposes of the conflict. Planning for the eventual peace became his concern as early as the outbreak of the European war, when he declared on September 3, 1939, that "the influence of America should be consistent in seeking for humanity a final peace which will eliminate, so far as it is possible to do so, the continued use of force between nations." Formal discussions began the same month in the State Department, and the first of a number of committees was formed in December 1939 to consider problems of peace and reconstruction. Numerous private organizations, such as the Council on Foreign Relations, began work on these issues, and their findings and recommendations often proved helpful to the government and to the development of a nation-wide feeling that the United States should participate in some kind of international body to prevent war.[6] Within weeks after the Pearl Harbor attack the President accelerated official planning by approving a request from Secretary Hull to establish an Advisory Committee on Post-War Foreign Policy.[7] Composed of members drawn from inside and outside the government, the committee spawned subcommittees and even special interim committees, with both regular and temporary participants. No publicity was given this committee or its activities for fear that it might give the impression of a protracted struggle and tend to lower morale.

The work of these committees embraced the entire spectrum of the postwar scene, and the Subcommittee on Security Problems was assigned, as one of its tasks, the formulation of terms for a cessation of hostilities with the various antagonists. Chairing this subcommittee was Norman H. Davis, one of America's most experienced diplomats. Successful in business and government, Davis had served both Republican and Democratic presidents. Among his many previous assignments were those of Assistant and Under Secretary of State, head of the United States delegation to the World Conference on the Reduction of Armaments at Geneva under Hoover and Roosevelt and chief of the American delegation to the Brussels Conference on the Far East in 1937. Currently president of the Coun-

6. Robert A. Divine, *Second Chance: The Triumph of Internationalism in America During World War II* (New York, 1967).
7. The request is dated December 22, 1941, and the approval is dated December 28, 1941.

cil on Foreign Relations and chairman of the American Red Cross, his qualifications for the post were exemplary. Of equal or greater significance was his long-time friendship with Roosevelt, which allowed him direct access to the source of decision.[8]

The Subcommittee on Security Problems began its deliberations on the method and the terms by which the war should be concluded on May 6, 1942. In dealing with method, a distinction was drawn between an armistice and an unconditional surrender. Both provided for a cessation of hostilities, with the former being negotiated and the latter being imposed. The members soon accepted the premise that unconditional surrender would be demanded of the principal enemy governments with the possible exception of Italy, which might be induced to withdraw from the war on the basis of a negotiated armistice. Subsequent meetings found the subcommittee considering alternatives which might be dictated by unforeseen contingencies, the need to prepare a document acceptable to the other major allies, and the advisability of terms relating to "purely military matters." While it was understood that conditions must be included to indicate the disposition of enemy forces, the release of prisoners, and the like, it was agreed that provisions should not embrace political affairs. Although such topics were within the purview of the Subcommittee, it was felt that their inclusion might have an adverse effect on the negotiations for a final peace treaty.

On May 20, 1942, Davis reported to the subcommittee that he had discussed its activities with the President and found him in agreement with the method adopted for terminating the conflict with the major Axis Powers. Thus Roosevelt, eight months prior to the announcement at Casablanca, pri-

8. The number of these committees established for postwar planning, their composition, the multitude of problems they dealt with, the vast amount of work they did, and the studies and recommendations they produced are astounding. The standard work is Harley A. Notter, *Postwar Foreign Policy Preparation, 1939–1945* (Washington, D.C., 1949), written by one of the State Department participants.

vately acknowledged his predilection for unconditional surrender. At least one of his reasons may have been consistent with an opinion shared by the subcommittee. As expressed by one of the members, Assistant Secretary of State Breckinridge Long, and recorded in the Minutes, "We are fighting this war because we did not have an unconditional surrender at the end of the last one." [9] This interpretation of the origin or cause of World War II, whether historically accurate or not, was partially responsible for the unconditional surrender doctrine. The truth or falsity of an opinion often has little correlation with the amount of influence it exerts.

But planning for enemy capitulation may have seemed a bit premature in light of the existing military situation, for the Axis Powers in the early summer of 1942 were at the pinnacle of their success. Japan had overrun Southeast Asia and the western Pacific; Germany dominated Europe, her spring offensive had driven into the Caucasus, and Marshal Rommel was pursuing the badly mauled British forces into Egypt. The time was scarcely propitious for an injection of the explosive issue of specific postwar aspirations into the Allied councils when crucial decisions on military strategy were imperative. Deferring a consideration of the details of peace assumed even greater significance in view of the fact that the three leaders of the United Nations realized that they were not all fighting for the same thing.

The American goals, along with the laudable ideals which permeated Roosevelt's public utterances, were readily discernible. First, to destroy the governments of the Axis nations, whose activities jeopardized the safety of the United States, the Western Hemisphere, and the entire world. Second, to establish a peace to demonstrate that aggression did not pay. Third, to eradicate injustices stemming from the Treaty of

9. The foregoing paragraphs are based on Minutes of the Subcommittee on Security Problems, in files of the Subcommittee, Department of State. These files also contain drafts of surrender documents, historical analyses, and other materials.

Versailles which had provided an excuse for aggression. Fourth, to create some kind of world order to enforce common standards of conduct among nations and halt aggression at its source. The President also sought to eliminate colonialism wherever possible, and for him the liberation and self-determination of peoples applied both to the Axis and Allied nations.

The British objectives were not so well defined, and Churchill frequently was subjected to criticism for not spelling out what the nation was fighting for. On one occasion, while being badgered in Parliament, he responded, "You asked, what is our aim? I can answer in one word: It is victory, victory at all costs, victory in spite of all terror, victory however hard and long the road may be." Typical Churchillian eloquence perhaps, but the destruction of Nazi ambition and power appeared to be an acceptable goal for domestic consumption under the circumstances. The more substantive ramifications of "victory" may have escaped the general public and some members of Parliament, and the Prime Minister was not anxious to tie his hands by previous declarations when the time came to deal with specifics. He could accept the principles incorporated in the Atlantic Charter and the Declaration of the United Nations because, in his opinion, they were sufficiently vague to permit almost any type of application. What Churchill wanted—and in this he was supported by his War Cabinet—was revealed in the position taken by the government since 1939. Britain did not go to war against Germany in order to save Poland but to prevent Hitler from establishing hegemony over Europe, and, because of the Axis alliance, to eliminate the threat to British overseas holdings by Italy and Japan. The military imperatives required American and Russian assistance, and the postwar situation demanded their collaboration. The preservation of the British Empire and the minimization of conditions which would jeopardize its continuance were the basic war aims of the government, the criteria against which all military and political decisions were measured. Operating within this context, Churchill's views clashed more often with those of Roosevelt than they did with those of Stalin. Foreign Secretary Anthony Eden might complain that "Mr. Churchill did not like to give his time to anything not exclusively concerned with the conduct of the war," [10] but the King's First Minister never lost sight of his primary responsibility even though his actions may have been misdirected.

The Russian aims were more clearly defined, and they became obvious at an early stage. The Soviet Union had joined with Germany in the partition of Poland in September of 1939 and soon incorporated its eastern area into the White Russian and Ukrainian Soviet Republics. In July 1940 the Baltic nations of Latvia, Lithuania, and Estonia were absorbed, and Rumania was induced to cede Bessarabia and Northern Bukovina. The German assault on June 22, 1941, brought an apparent change in the Russian attitude, for the following month the Kremlin and the Polish government-in-exile in London signed an agreement which specified in Article 1: "The Government of the U.S.S.R. recognizes the Soviet-German treaties of 1939 as to territorial changes in Poland as having lost their validity. The Polish Government declares Poland is not bound by any agreement with any third power which is directed against the U.S.S.R." [11] During the fall of 1941 the hard-pressed Russians sought an arrangement with Great Britain on postwar settlements but were rebuffed with the explanation that nothing more specific than the provisions of the Atlantic Charter could be discussed without the participation of the United States, which continued to urge the British government to avoid any specific commitments.[12] The Russians repeatedly voiced their fear of an "Anglo-American peace" with Germany at the expense of the Soviet Union, and in early December 1941 Foreign Secretary Anthony Eden journeyed to Moscow in an effort to quiet these suspicions. Handed a

10. *The Memoirs of Anthony Eden: The Reckoning* (Boston, 1965), 512.

11. *FR, 1941,* I, 243.

12. Sir Llewellyn Woodward, *British Foreign Policy in the Second World War* (London, 1962), 158–59.

draft proposal for an alliance which included a recognition of Russia's "1941 frontiers with Finland, the Baltic States and Roumania," Eden protested that he had no authority to consider such matters and referred the proposal to London, where a decision was delayed pending the return of Churchill from Washington. The British government, convinced that the treaty was a military necessity, began a campaign to persuade Roosevelt to withdraw his opposition to postwar territorial adjustments. The British contended that the Soviets could control these areas after the war in any case, that Russia would be the most powerful nation on the Continent after the war and her good will was essential, that Britain actually was contributing relatively little in the war against Germany, and that the Russians might feel a rejection of these war aims would indicate that Britain and the Soviet Union were not fighting for the same thing and a peaceful settlement with Germany would be to the Russian interest. Roosevelt firmly and consistently opposed the boundary provisions of the treaty, was not swayed by the British arguments, felt that a settlement of territorial questions was premature, and that those proposed appeared to be in violation of the Atlantic Charter. Unable to induce either ally to budge on the issue, "The War Cabinet," as the official British historian puts it, "now had to choose between giving way to the Russians or to the Americans." The Cabinet chose to give way to the Soviets, and decided on a counter offer that would recognize Russia's borders as of 1940 except for Poland.[13] The Russian response was not encouraging, and when Foreign Minister Molotov arrived in London en route to the United States he was presented with a new British version which provided for a long-term alliance and postwar cooperation while ignoring completely the question of boundaries. Surprisingly, after an initial summary rejection, Molotov accepted the treaty, which was signed on May 26, 1942.

13. *Ibid.*, 193. For correspondence and memoranda of conversations on this subject, see *FR, 1942*, III, 490–562.

Just why the Kremlin leaders dropped their previous demands was not revealed, although the German spring offensive may have convinced the Russians that a formal military alliance had its advantages. A more plausible explanation, however, might be found in the constant American objections to any pact embodying territorial adjustments. Britain had been willing, albeit reluctantly, to incur American wrath and ignore previous assurances given Washington in order to conciliate Moscow. But Stalin, after months of British resistance and a growing awareness of American intractability, abandoned the contentious provisions of the treaty. Thus American objections were instrumental in Britain's delay and her refusal to accept all of Russia's demands, and they were probably decisive in bringing about the Soviet reversal. Stalin had no desire to provoke the enmity of the United States at this crucial juncture of the war, and he may have been aware that the President was not so apprehensive about a Russian "defection" as was the Prime Minister.[14]

Further complicating Anglo-American relations during the early months of 1942 was the controversy over where and how the Western Allies should strike their first major blow against Axis Europe. Tentative plans for a North African venture (GYMNAST) were dropped when it became apparent that the Vichy government would not cooperate and the British offensive in Libya had failed. The American planners now intensified their studies of a cross-channel attack from England to the northern coast of France to be launched in September if the Russian front were in danger of collapse, or in April 1943 if the Russians held out. Roosevelt endorsed the proposal, which met with his desire for "a new front on the European Continent." [15] Meeting in London with their British counter-

14. In a conversation on May 29, 1942, Molotov told Roosevelt that the frontier problem had been omitted from the treaty in deference to "British preference and to what he understood to be the attitude of the President." *FR, 1942*, III, 569.

15. Maurice Matloff and Edwin M. Snell, *Strategic Planning for Coalition Warfare, 1941–1942* (Washington, D.C., 1953), 183–84.

parts during the second week of April, the American representatives secured the approval of the British Chiefs of Staff and the Prime Minister for BOLERO, the United States build-up in England in preparation for SLEDGEHAMMER, the contingency operation, and ROUNDUP, the massive invasion scheduled for spring 1943. The President, subjected to strident appeals for the allocation of resources to other theaters in this global war, assigned top priority to preparations for the assault on Europe. As he put it, "I do not want 'Bolero' slowed down." [16]

Yet the President seemed unwilling to wait until 1943 for some kind of engagement of American forces on the Continent, and he sought "action in 1942—not 1943." [17] After meetings with Soviet Foreign Minister Molotov in Washington at the end of May and in early June, the President authorized a public statement which read: "In the course of the conversations full understanding was reached with regard to the urgent tasks of creating a second front in Europe in 1942." [18] Whether Roosevelt intended this "understanding" to constitute a commitment for mounting a cross-channel attack in 1942 is not clear, although his impatience for involvement on the Continent would so indicate. On the other hand, he was anxious to provide greater moral and material support for the Russians who were bearing the brunt of the Axis military onslaught, and a public announcement of the "urgent tasks" could have been viewed as a propaganda device designed to reassure the Allies and create apprehension among the enemies. British assurances of a second front in 1942, given to Molotov earlier, while he was in London, had been hedged with qualifications. Possibly reflecting a growing British skepticism about the feasibility of the venture, these reservations gave the impression

16. Letter to General Marshall, May 6, 1942, reproduced *ibid.*, 220.
17. *Ibid.*, 222.
18. Robert E. Sherwood, *Roosevelt and Hopkins: An Intimate History* (revised edition, New York, 1950), 577. A detailed account of these conversations is contained *ibid.*, 556–79.

of a less binding commitment than that made by the President. Soon after Molotov left Washington an emissary from Churchill arrived. Lord Louis Mountbatten was charged with persuading the Americans to drop SLEDGEHAMMER and engage in a less formidable operation more compatible with British aspirations. When the President appeared sympathetic to a revival of the North African project, his advisers strenuously objected on the grounds that it would be an indecisive diversionary effort and delay ROUNDUP. Then the Prime Minister and his staff returned to Washington and the strategic debate continued in a series of meetings at all levels. As the controversy reached its crescendo a new ingredient was added which put the issue in a different light. In June the British Eighth Army suffered a resounding defeat in Libya. Tobruk fell, and the entire British position in the Middle East was in danger. Resources immediately were allocated in an effort to avert a complete disaster, but the meeting concluded with a reaffirmation of ROUNDUP in 1943. News of the "incredible" American victory at Midway in early June led to a slight increase in support for the Pacific theater to permit what Admiral Ernest J. King called the "tactically offensive, strategically defensive" policy, but halting the Japanese thrust supported the contention that no substantive resources needed to be diverted from the planned cross-channel operation. The major military effort remained as contemplated by the American planners—the invasion of Europe.

It was Churchill who once observed that the only thing worse than fighting with allies is fighting without them. On July 8, 1942, the British Government advised Washington that SLEDGEHAMMER would not be undertaken and urged that North Africa be the target. Both General Marshall and Admiral King reacted vigorously against this proposal, maintaining that it would be indecisive and diversionary, and would delay the imperative European assault. Presenting their views in a memorandum to the President, they recommended that if the British persisted in their attitude, the United States should

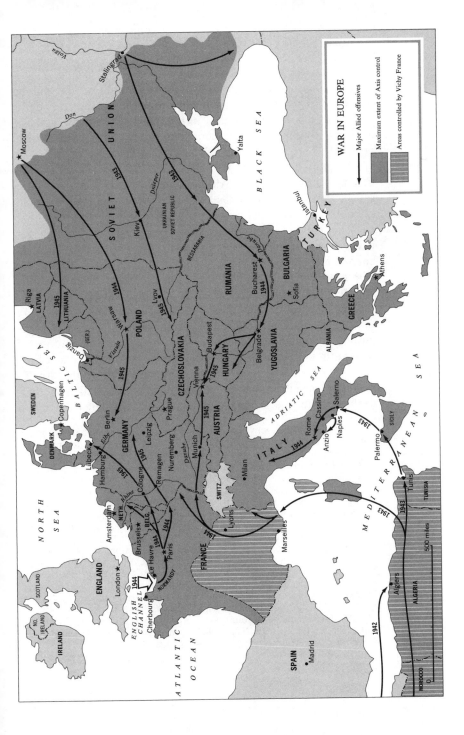

WAR IN EUROPE

Major Allied offensives
Maximum extent of Axis control
Areas controlled by Vichy France

alter its "Europe first" strategy and concentrate on the war in the Pacific. Roosevelt was unwilling to jeopardize the close relationship with Britain and, in lieu of an ultimatum, sent his advisers to London in a vain attempt to change the British position. The discouraged American delegation returned to Washington and began the implementation of TORCH, the new name for the North African invasion, having derived little satisfaction from Churchill's assurance that the operation would not delay the projected cross-channel attack.[19]

The indirect, peripheral strategy espoused by Britain for many generations had prevailed. Instead of striking at the main enemy forces, the North African operation was designed to eliminate the Axis threat in the Middle East, help clear the Mediterranean to secure the British lifeline, and provide a base for the subsequent invasions of Sicily and Italy and secure the latter's surrender.[20] It did not strike at the heart of Axis power, it opened the Western Allies to Russian allegations of bad faith in regard to a second front, it delayed the cross-channel invasion by more than a year, it placed the Anglo-American negotiators in a weaker bargaining position in their dealings with the Russians, and it gave the Soviet Army a

19. This was merely one of a number of occasions when the President overruled his advisers on military strategy, and tends to invalidate the contention that "As Commander in Chief he left major military planning decisions in the hands of the Joint Chiefs and military planners." James MacGregor Burns, *Roosevelt: The Soldier of Freedom, 1940–1945* (New York, 1970), 494. The former Chief Historian of the Department of the Army, Kent Roberts Greenfield, has listed more than twenty instances in which the President rejected the recommendations of his military advisers and a dozen cases where he instituted operations. Kent Roberts Greenfield, *American Strategy in World War II: A Reconsideration* (Baltimore, 1963), Chapter III. On this question, see also William R. Emerson, "F.D.R. (1941–1945)," in Ernest R. May, ed., *The Ultimate Decision: The President as Commander in Chief* (New York, 1960), 133–77; and Maurice Matloff, "Franklin Delano Roosevelt as War Leader," in Harry L. Coles, ed., *Total War and Cold War: Problems in Civilian control of the Military* (Columbus, Ohio, 1962), 42–65.

20. For a concise account, see Leo J. Meyer, "The Decision to Invade North Africa (TORCH) (1942)," in Kent Roberts Greenfield, ed., *Command Decisions* (New York, 1959), 129–53.

greater opportunity to overrun most of Eastern Europe. Assuming that the military conquest of territory and a greater contribution to victory over the common foe add weight to the demands of an ally, the question remains whether an Anglo-American landing on the western coast of France in 1943 would have been successful.

Hitler in the months and years following his mastery of Western and much of Eastern Europe strove to weld this area into a gigantic fortress. In exploiting these non-German nations for raw materials and labor, the Nazis marshalled the human, natural, and industrial resources of the Continent. So, in spite of the enormous drain on the Eastern front, Hitler's domain became more formidable as time went on. Similarly, the Anglo-American forces were not so well prepared in 1943 as they were in 1944, and control of the air had not been established. Enemy communication facilities were relatively intact, industrial resources had suffered little, and the Eastern front had yet to take a crucial toll. On the other hand, the German defenders were ill prepared to repulse a seaborne assault. They did not occupy all of France until the time of the North African Allied invasion, and as late as December 1943, when Rommel inspected defenses in the West, he found the beaches lightly guarded and only one combat-ready armored division available. In 1942 and 1943 the Wehrmacht divisions in France were few, composed largely of trainees or troops recouping from or deemed unfit for service in Russia. Certain ports in occupied France were heavily fortified, as the bloody Dieppe probe revealed,[21] but essentially the Germans were not prepared to repulse or contain the large-scale assault envisioned by the American planners. Only a drastic reallocation of forces from the Eastern front could have prevented the Allied thrust from succeeding, and such a move would have opened the Nazi stronghold to the Soviets. The Atlantic Wall boasted of by Hitler may never have been, as Marshal von

21. In a commando raid on the French port of Dieppe, August 19, 1942, the Canadian and English attackers sustained 50 percent casualties.

Rundstedt put it, an "illusion," but the defenses against an Allied landing and its exploitation changed from token to formidable as Anglo-American operations were concentrated on the Mediterranean.[22]

This diversion of effort delayed the invasion of Western Europe by at least a year, enabled the Soviets to occupy more of the Continent and make a greater contribution to the winning of the war, and enhanced their bargaining power not only at the later conferences but in earlier discussions dealing with occupation zones, borders, control of "liberated" nations, reparations, and the like. If the cross-channel invasion had been implemented as originally planned for spring 1943, the Anglo-American troops would have been engaging the main enemy forces, making a greater contribution to the winning of the war, and occupying vital territory at the time when postwar settlements were discussed. And it should be noted that, as will become apparent, many of the controversial questions formally resolved at the Yalta Conference in 1945 were actually dealt with and tentatively settled at Tehran in December 1943, some six months before D-Day in Europe.[23] So the British strategy which prevailed, the peripheral move into the Mediterranean rather than the American direct assault on Europe, proved detrimental to the achievement of the political objectives of the war. The American plan would have placed the Western Allies in a stronger position to secure the kind of peace they wanted, with a greater voice in the composition of governments and the conduct of free elections in liberated nations.

22. German preparations for defense in the West are covered in Gordon Harrison, *Cross-Channel Attack* (Washington, D.C., 1951), Chapter IV; and Friedrich Ruge, "German Naval Operations on D-Day," in *D-Day: The Normandy Invasion in Retrospect* (Lawrence, Kansas, 1971), 149–69. These volumes, the latter consisting of essays by acknowledged experts, are indispensable for an understanding of the assault.
23. William M. Franklin, "Yalta Viewed From Tehran," in Daniel R. Beaver, ed., *Some Pathways in Twentieth Century History: Essays in Honor of Reginald Charles McGrane* (Detroit, 1969), 253–301.

The delay further added to the Kremlin's distrust of the Western Allies, who were suspected of deliberately allowing the Germans to bleed the Russians and thereby weaken this communist country. Although there is no evidence to justify these suspicions, the postponement of the cross-channel invasion threatened to disrupt the coalition. Only elaborate explanations by Churchill and Roosevelt were able to pacify Stalin, who probably never forgave what he considered a breach of trust. Whether this incident marked the beginning of the Cold War is a matter of definition, but it doubtless served to increase Russian qualms about the motives of their Western colleagues.

The North African operation involved the invasion of neutral French territory, provided an opportunity for a meeting at Casablanca between Roosevelt and Churchill in January 1943 to determine the next military venture, and inadvertently supplied both the occasion and motives for announcing the "unconditional surrender" policy. As the troops streamed ashore, the President wrote Marshal Henri Philippe Pétain, head of the French government at Vichy, that the Allied occupation of Algeria was necessary to forestall Axis plans for the area. The Marshal responded by severing relations with the United States and directing his forces to fight the invaders. A brief resistance was ended by an armistice negotiated with Admiral Jean-François Darlan, a high official of the Vichy government who happened to be in Algiers at the time. This "deal" with a "fascist collaborator" was loudly denounced in the United States, and Roosevelt, stung by the outcry, sought for some means of countering this adverse reaction.[24] Contributing to his anxiety, at Casablanca General Marshall's plea for a revival of ROUNDUP (whose code name later became OVERLORD) was overcome by British insistence on a continuation

24. The administration also was subjected to criticism for maintaining relations with the totalitarian Franco government in Spain. Yet both Washington and London were determined to prevent Spain from joining the Axis as a belligerent, providing military assistance short of war, or supplying strategic materials. See Herbert Feis, *The Spanish Story: Franco and the Nations at War* (New York, 1948, 1966).

of activity in the Mediterranean with cumulative objectives of capturing Sicily, knocking Italy out of the war, and drawing Turkey in on the side of the Allies. Further delay in engaging the main German forces, and vulnerability to the charge of temporizing with enemy puppets gave impetus to the advisability of an unequivocal assertion of surrender terms, with "unconditional" as a simple categorical modifier.

Some of the myths concerning the origins of this doctrine have been dispelled earlier in this narrative, and it may be well to deal with a few others that have been perpetuated. The President, as has been indicated, had these terms in mind for some time, and he so indicated in a meeting with the Joint Chiefs of Staff as late as January 7 just before leaving for Casablanca.[25] Churchill's contention that he "heard the words 'Unconditional Surrender' for the first time from the President's lips at the [press] Conference," [26] was later corrected by the Prime Minister himself. Elliot Roosevelt's assertion that "the phrase 'unconditional surrender' was born" at a luncheon on January 23 is obviously in error, although it contributed to the legend that the doctrine was an off-the-cuff remark by the President.[27]

One criticism of the unconditional surrender policy is directed more to its promulgation than to its adoption. Announcing publicly such uncompromising terms, it is contended, could not help but stiffen enemy resistance and render more difficult efforts to halt the fighting. Roosevelt, by promulgating this doctrine at a press conference following the Casablanca meeting, is held responsible for what some consider a politically and militarily unwise declaration of aims. Unhappily for the

25. As recorded in the Joint Chiefs of Staff Minutes, "The President said he was going to speak to Mr. Churchill about the advisability of informing Mr. Stalin that the United Nations were to continue on until they reach Berlin, and that their only terms would be unconditional surrender." *FR, The Conference at Washington, 1941–1942, and Casablanca, 1943,* 506.
26. Sherwood, *Roosevelt and Hopkins,* 696.
27. Elliott Roosevelt, *As He Saw It* (New York, 1946), 117.

President's critics, it was the Prime Minister who initiated this action.

Meeting with Churchill and the members of the Combined Chiefs of Staff on January 18, 1943, Roosevelt introduced the question of press releases and photographs. Responding, the Prime Minister

suggested that at the same time we release a statement to the effect that the United Nations are resolved to pursue the war to the bitter end, neither party relaxing in its efforts until the unconditional surrender of Germany and Japan has been achieved. He said that before issuing such a statement, he would like to consult with his colleagues in London.[28]

The War Cabinet reacted enthusiastically and urged the inclusion of Italy, being "convinced that the effect on the Italians would be good." [29] Originally intended to be included in the final press release and actually incorporated in an early draft which specified "the simple formula of an unconditional surrender by Germany and Japan" with the insertion of *Italy* in Churchill's handwriting, the pronouncement was to be reserved for oral delivery by the President.[30]

The press corps met with the two leaders on January 24, 1943, in an atmosphere of relaxed cordiality and an eager anticipation of startling revelations. As the correspondents clustered around Roosevelt and Churchill to hear reports on the progress of the war and plans for future operations, they witnessed an unrehearsed handshake between the two rivals for leadership of the free French forces, General Henri Giraud and Major General Charles de Gaulle. The President, in his opening remarks and speaking from notes, declared that "peace can come to the world only by the total elimination of German and Japanese war power." He then went on to say:

Some of you Britishers know the old story—we had a General called U. S. Grant. His name was Ulysses Simpson Grant, but in

28. *FR, Conferences at Washington and Casablanca,* 635.
29. The dispatches and related information are in Sherwood, *Roosevelt and Hopkins,* 972–73.
30. *FR, Conferences at Washington and Casablanca,* 833–35.

my, and the Prime Minister's, early days he was called 'Unconditional Surrender' Grant. The elimination of German, Japanese and Italian war power means the unconditional surrender by Germany, Italy, and Japan. That means a reasonable assurance of future world peace. It does not mean the destruction of the population of Germany, Italy, or Japan, but it does mean the destruction of the philosophies in those countries which are based on conquest and the subjugation of other people.

The President then added, "this meeting is called the 'unconditional surrender' meeting." [31] The notes from which Roosevelt spoke read:

> The President and the Prime Minister, after a complete survey of the world war situation, are more than ever determined that peace can come to the world only by a total elimination of German and Japanese war power. This involves the simple formula of placing the objective of this war in terms of an unconditional surrender by Germany, Italy and Japan. Unconditional surrender by them means a reasonable assurance of world peace, for generations. Unconditional surrender means not the destruction of the German populace, nor of the Italian or Japanese populace, but does mean the destruction of a philosophy in Germany, Italy and Japan which is based on the conquest and subjugation of other peoples. [32]

Just why the unconditional surrender statement contained in Roosevelt's notes for the press conference was not included in the official press release, as originally intended and as incorporated in the earlier draft, is not clear. Nonetheless, the record indicates that the two leaders had agreed to a public declaration of this policy. Obviously, Roosevelt and Churchill changed their minds about including the declaration in the

31. *Ibid.*, 727.
32. *Ibid.*, 837. A slightly different version appears in Rosenman, *1943: The Tide Turns*, 37–45. Rosenman erroneously says, "This was the President's own statement, made at the press conference without prior consultation with Churchill, but of course was strongly supported by Churchill." *Ibid.*, 47. The assertion in the British official history that "The President, however, without previously consulting the Prime Minister, used the words in a press conference" is absurd (Woodward, *British Foreign Policy in the Second World War*, 436). Woodward is outspokenly critical of the announcement and the policy. See *ibid.*, 437, footnote.

press release and decided instead to incorporate it in the President's opening remarks, possibly because it would receive better news coverage and have a more dramatic impact.

The reasons for issuing this declaration as revealed by the record are doubtless incomplete, for both of these leaders were too experienced in the ways of war and of nations to be unaware of other advantages. The timing is especially relevant, for it followed a conference in which future military operations were determined that would further postpone the promised second front in Western Europe. News of the delay could be expected to provoke another outburst of recriminations from the Russians and renew their suspicions that the Anglo-American combination was conspiring to weaken its Communist partner, and, at a propitious moment, negotiate peace with Germany in spite of agreements not to do so. This formal announcement specifically rejecting any deal for a termination of hostilities could serve to compensate for the disappointing news of further offensives in the Mediterranean and to reassure the Soviets concerning the intentions of their Western associates, who in turn would feel more confident of Stalin's intentions if he should subscribe to the formula.

Yet it was the specific nature of the declaration that led to so much criticism, not especially at the time but later. It was well enough for the United Nations to sign a document pledging "complete victory," for the Congress to direct the President to "bring the conflict to a successful conclusion," and have him declare the nation's dedication to "final victory," "absolute victory," and the like, and for Churchill to proclaim "victory at all costs." This terminology was conventional and consistent with the type of exhortation normally employed by governments when waging war. Sufficient to engender domestic enthusiasm and provide a common military goal over which allies could scarcely quarrel, these phrases allowed for flexibility in implementation and, in their ambiguity, offered hope to the enemy. The unequivocal explicitness of the Casablanca announcement probably brought despair to the hearts of the Axis peoples, but it also provided their masters with an effective propaganda device for exhorting them to greater sacrifice in order to avert what was portrayed as extinction. Some Allied military leaders became dissatisfied with the formula, for while it presented them with a clear-cut military objective it was, in Admiral Ernest J. King's words, "unduly rigid," and ·it tended to "discourage thought." [33] Eisenhower later claimed that the "slogan" caused the Germans to fight longer and harder and lengthened the war by sixty to ninety days, and he quoted General Marshall as saying the policy was a "mistake." [34] Although the military commanders may have felt hampered in their dealings with the opposition, it is unlikely that the doctrine affected the terms by which they could accept the capitulation of the enemy armed forces, whose "conditional" surrender was clearly unacceptable.

The statement, it must be remembered, called for "The elimination of German, Japanese and Italian war power," which meant "the unconditional surrender by Germany, Italy, and Japan." It did not mean, the President explained, "the destruction of the population of Germany, Italy, or Japan." Subsequently, the President and the Prime Minister repeatedly gave assurances of humane treatment for the people of these nations, and this information was disseminated by short-wave radio and leaflets dropped by aircraft. The treatment accorded Italy after her armistice/surrender on September 3, 1943, gave no evidence of a Carthaginian peace, although admittedly there were extenuating circumstances which will be mentioned later.[35] Clearly implied in the doctrine, however, was a free hand in determining the fate of the govern-

33. E. J. King and W. M. Whitehill, *Fleet Admiral King—A Naval Record* (New York, 1952), 425.

34. Eisenhower interview reported in *Washington Post,* December 21, 1964.

35. Churchill hoped Germany would be impressed by the leniency shown Italy. See Churchill to Sir Alexander Cadogan, April 19, 1944, printed in Winston S. Churchill, *Closing the Ring* (*The Second World War,* Vol. V) (Boston, 1951), 706.

ment and the nation. The word "unconditional" had an ominous ring about it. The vanquished were to be at the complete mercy of the victors, whose appetite for vengeance might be insatiable after the horrors and sufferings inflicted by the Axis powers. The Germans, too, could recall the experience of the First World War when, as many were convinced, the Armistice terms had been violated by the Allied and Associated Powers at Versailles. Of what value were prior agreements after military resistance had collapsed and the triumphant foe was able to impose his will without restraint? Foreign Secretary Anthony Eden could quote with approval a passage from *Mein Kampf* in which Hitler said, "A wise victor will, if possible, always impose his claim on the defeated people stage by stage." [36] Elected governments were especially susceptible to public clamor for the punishment of an adversary whose evil nature and inhuman behavior had been portrayed so vividly. Memories of the previous experience may have been more responsible for German recalcitrance than the threatening words uttered by the leaders of two nations whose military prospects at the moment were not too bright.

The Soviet government, which had not been consulted prior to the announcement, did not formally endorse the doctrine until a foreign ministers' conference was held in Moscow, October 18 to November 1, 1943, between Hull, Eden, and Molotov. The latter proved a congenial, cooperative host, and the meeting produced a "Declaration of Four Nations on General Security" containing a pledge "to continue hostilities against those Axis powers with which they respectively are at war until such powers have laid down their arms on the basis of unconditional surrender." [37] While the phrase implied the inclusion of Axis satellites and indicated a broadening of the

36. Eden, *The Reckoning,* 52–53.
37. *FR, 1943,* I, 755. Although China was not represented at this "Tripartite Conference," both Hull and Eden contended that China should be included in the Declaration. Molotov finally consented, and the Chinese ambassador to Moscow signed the document on behalf of his government.

Casablanca formula, there seemed to be no clear understanding on the question, and in practice the doctrine was not incorporated in the surrender terms for Germany's other European allies.[38]

38. *Ibid.*, 681; *FR, 1943*, III, 287, footnote 3. The United States sought to place Finland in a separate category.

4

First Surrenders and
Postwar Settlements

THE FIRST TEST of the highly publicized unconditional surrender policy was provided by the capitulation of Italy. Armistice terms formulated in Washington and London during the spring of 1943 tried to anticipate the outcome of an Allied invasion of the country, including the possibility of internal revolution and the prospect that the Nazis would defend the Peninsula even if the Italian government surrendered. Further complicating the planners' task was the Allied desire to utilize Italy as a base for prosecuting the war against Germany, hopefully with the cooperation of the Italian government. Initial proposals submitted by the British were unacceptable to the Americans because they did not constitute an unconditional surrender, and by the time of the Sicily invasion the two governments had not reached agreement on what should be demanded of Italy when her anticipated defeat occurred.[1]

The resignation of Prime Minister Benito Mussolini on July 25 stirred Allied hopes for a quick collapse and prompted vigorous efforts to formulate armistice terms. The President,

1. Albert N. Garland and Howard McGaw Smyth, *Sicily and the Surrender of Italy* (Washington, 1965), 25–26. For material concerning the Italian armistice/surrender, see *FR, 1943,* II, 314–445; *FR, The Conferences at Washington and Quebec, 1943,* 516 *passim;* and Alfred D. Chandler, Jr., and Stephen E. Ambrose, eds., *The Papers of Dwight David Eisenhower: The War Years* (5 vols., Baltimore, 1970), II, 1287–1397, and III, 1401–7.

exhilarated by the news, wired Churchill, "It is my thought that we should come as close as possible to unconditional surrender followed by good treatment of the Italian populace. But I think also that the head devil should be surrendered together with his chief partners in crime." [2] In a Fireside Chat three days later, the President reaffirmed that "our terms to Italy are still the same as our terms to Germany and Japan— 'unconditional surrender.' " [3] The War Cabinet, Churchill advised, "are quite clear that we ought not to broadcast armistice terms to the enemy. It is for their responsible government to ask formally for an armistice on the basis of our principle of unconditional surrender." [4] Then followed an exchange of messages between Washington and London in an attempt to reach agreement on details, with occasional efforts to clear developments with Moscow. At one point Stalin protested about being kept in the dark, but subsequently he approved the terms arrived at, authorized Eisenhower to sign the armistice document, and did not insist that a representative of the Soviet Union be present.[5]

The contention that the "publicly proclaimed demand for unconditional surrender" prevented an earlier peace with Mussolini appears to be without foundation.[6] The Allied leaders were determined to eliminate the dictator and the Fascist governmental structure irrespective of the slogan, and it was unlikely that Mussolini would accept a settlement which destroyed him and what he stood for. Evidently the king and his advisers were aware of this major obstacle to an armistice, and by forcing Mussolini's resignation they opened the road to negotiation. Roosevelt's willingness to bend the formula was consistent with the British view, although agreement on specifics did consume a great deal of time and effort.

2. *FR, 1943*, II, 332.
3. Rosenman, *1943: The Tide Turns,* 327.
4. *FR, 1943*, II, 336.
5. *Ibid.,* 353, 357.
6. Garland and Smyth, *Sicily and the Surrender of Italy,* 44, 51.

In the middle of all these intricate arrangements was General Eisenhower. Given the responsibility for dealing with representatives of the Italian government and concluding an armistice, Eisenhower found it equally troublesome to negotiate with his superiors. Being compelled to clear every detail with Washington was difficult enough, but he was constantly beset with interference from the British, who insisted on sharing in the deliberations. The Italians, on their part, were more frightened of the Germans than they were of the Allies, and they demanded guarantees of adequate protection against their erstwhile partner and acceptance as a co-belligerent. Eventually two surrender documents were hammered out by the Allies, a brief "short-term" document and a more detailed "long-term" instrument. The former, which provided for a subsequent signature of the latter, was signed on September 3, 1943, by the Italian emissary, who probably was gratified by the absence of an "unconditional surrender" stipulation. To his chagrin, later the same day he was presented with the second document which contained the clause "The Italian Land, Sea and Air Forces wherever located, hereby surrender unconditionally." After a series of protests, further exchanges, and face-saving statements by the American representatives, the more comprehensive terms were finally signed on September 29. This document itself was modified by a protocol signed November 9, which deleted the word "unconditionally." The Italian government, striving to maintain itself, combat the Germans, and collaborate with the Allies, eventually managed to eliminate the most offensive part of the surrender text.[7]

The Italian armistice did not represent an unconditional surrender by the government as postulated by the Casablanca declaration and subsequent pronouncements of the American

7. Robert J. Quinlan, "The Italian Armistice," in Stein, *American Civil-Military Decisions,* 280. Eisenhower, on September 8, announced in a radio address that Italy had surrendered unconditionally, and called on Italian support to "help eject the German aggressor from Italian soil. . . ." The Allied invasion of Italy centered around Salerno began early on September 9.

and British leaders. Evidently it came "close" enough to satisfy
the President, who was aware of the military advantages of
Italian defection from the Axis and collaboration with the
Allies. But two of what might be considered the President's
indispensable conditions were met. First, the Fascist dictator
Mussolini had been toppled, and his removal satisfied the
declared aim of eliminating the aggressor governments. Second, the Italian armed forces were surrendered unconditionally. Both Roosevelt and Churchill had been inclined to place
Italy in a separate category from Germany and Japan, although
publicly they had made no such distinction. The Italian situation was unique, and the same considerations were not likely
to prevail in the case of the other Axis Powers, but the inclusion of the formula did enable the President to proclaim that
the first major foe to capitulate had done so unconditionally.[8]
The presence of numerous "conditions" in both the long and
short-term documents of a military as well as a nonmilitary
character revealed a disposition toward flexibility in interpret-
ing and applying the doctrine. Whether the example would
be lost on the remaining antagonists was unknown, although
Churchill hoped it would be taken to heart by the Germans.[9]
The President, however, was not inclined to relax his demands
toward that nation which he considered primarily responsible
for the current holocaust.

In any event, the unconditional surrender formula could
eliminate the intricate and time-consuming haggling over details, even though it did not do so in the case of Italy. What
the formula could not eliminate was the necessity for specific
terms in any armistice or surrender document. Essential items
to be covered included the disarmament and disposition of
troops, the release of prisoners, the administration of internal
affairs, and a host of other "housekeeping" details. Yet it was
reasonable to assume that many of the considerations present

8. Rosenman, *1943: The Tide Turns,* 392.
9. Churchill, *Closing the Ring,* 706.

in the Italian surrender would not prevail in subsequent capitulations where the objectives of the Western Allies did not embrace collaboration. At the same time the Anglo-American leaders were probably alerted to potential difficulties with the Soviet Union, which had insisted on consultation but renounced participation in the negotiations. The precedent established of allowing those nations most directly involved in the military and armistice activities to control the arrangements for a conclusion of hostilities was not lost on the Russians, who might expect to be accorded reciprocal discretion under similar circumstances.

Russian dissatisfaction with the unconditional surrender policy, which had been endorsed in the Declaration of Four Nations, was voiced by Stalin at the Tehran Conference in November 1943. Contending that it could only provoke more determined German resistance, he advocated the promulgation of specific terms regardless of their severity.[10] Apparently Churchill agreed, and the British Foreign Office suggested that the phrase "prompt surrender" be substituted.[11] Subsequent efforts by the Russians and the British to induce Roosevelt to modify the doctrine were only partially successful, for he insisted on the "principle" being retained although he conceded that exceptions might be made in "the application of it in specific cases." [12] Finally he did consent to the elimination of the term in propaganda directed toward the German satellite states, and on May 12, 1944, a joint statement by the United States, Great Britain, and the Soviet Union declared that Hungary, Rumania, Bulgaria, and Finland, "still have it within their power, by withdrawing from the war and ceasing their collaboration with Germany and by resisting the forces of Nazism by every possible means, to shorten the European

10. *FR, Conferences at Cairo and Tehran, 1943, 513.*
11. Cordell Hull, *The Memoirs of Cordell Hull* (2 vols., New York, 1948), II, 1572.
12. *Ibid.,* 1577; *FR, 1944,* I, 592.

struggle, diminish their own ultimate sacrifices, and contribute to the Allied Victory." [13] The carrot now reinforced the stick by appealing to Germany's partners in a way reminiscent of the Italian experience, and it held out the promise of a modification of the letter if not the spirit or "principle" of the unconditional surrender dictum.

While this amplification of the policy did not contradict the Casablanca formula, it did modify the Declaration of Four Nations with one possible exception. Finland, an ally of Germany, was not regarded by the United States as technically one of the Axis Powers.[14] Within months following the joint appeal, Finland, Rumania, and Bulgaria sued for peace, although it would appear that they were influenced more by the deteriorating military situation than by the prospect of lenient terms. In each case a new government concluded the armistice, and in each case the Soviet Union played a dominant role in formulating the terms, negotiating the document, and administering affairs in the defeated nation. The notorious deal between Churchill and Stalin, whereby the former proposed

13. *The Memoirs of Cordell Hull,* II, 1580. In November 1944 Roosevelt, responding to an appeal from Eisenhower, asked Churchill about issuing a joint statement indicating that the Allies were not bent on destroying the German people or the nation. The Prime Minister, after consulting the War Cabinet, refused on the grounds that "the alteration of our tone" would increase resistance and raise enemy morale. Eisenhower agreed. Chandler and Ambrose, *The Papers of Dwight D. Eisenhower,* IV, 2312, 2318–19.

14. This distinction is based on a number of factors. The two nations did not go to war with each other; relations were maintained until June 30, 1944; Finland had continued payments on her World War I debt during the 1930s when other countries had defaulted, and the United States sympathized with Finland in her 1939–1940 war with Russia. Hull, in a press conference on July 26, 1943, placed Hungary, Rumania, and Bulgaria in the Axis category but referred to Finland as a "marginal case." *FR, 1943,* III, 287, footnote 8. A State Department memorandum of November 26, 1943, stated, "It seems to be a fact that Finland is not a signatory to the Tripartite pact and hence it is not an 'Axis Power,' though it may be an Axis 'satellite.'" *Ibid.,* 307. The United States was not a party to the armistice or the final peace treaty with Finland.

and the latter accepted an allocation of control in the Balkan states with Russia accorded 90 percent in Rumania and 75 percent in Bulgaria, occurred after the surrender of these two countries, but it probably conformed to the realities of the situation.[15] According to the Prime Minister, this arrangement was to prevail only during the war, but the occupation of these countries by Soviet troops gave the Russians a considerable advantage in determining the course of events. The Anglo-American authorities struggled in vain to secure a greater voice in the affairs of these nations as the Kremlin extended its influence throughout southeastern Europe.[16]

This division of responsibilities in the Balkans was not a sudden inspiration on the part of the Prime Minister. As early as May 1944 he reported to Roosevelt that the Russians were willing to accept political control in Rumania and allow the British to administer affairs in Greece. The President demurred, contending that the arrangement would divide the Balkans into "spheres of influence" and advocating "consultative machinery" to eliminate this danger. Churchill vigorously opposed what he called a "Committee" approach and warned of the unsettling effect of consultation and "a set of triangular or quadrangular telegrams." Finally the President reluctantly

15. Winston S. Churchill, *Triumph and Tragedy* (*The Second World War,* Vol. VI) (Boston, 1953), 227. This event took place on October 9, 1944. But as pointed out recently by one experienced diplomat, "The validity of any of the Stalin-Churchill discussions in October 1944 on percentage degree of influence in the Balkans remains unclear." (Charles E. Bohlen, *The Transformation of American Foreign Policy* [New York, 1969], 41, footnote).

16. Correspondence relating to negotiations for an armistice with the Hungarian government, concluded in Moscow, January 20, 1945, is in *FR, 1944,* III, 847–983; that relating to the armistice with Rumania, signed at Moscow, September 13, 1944, is in *FR, 1944,* IV, 133–232; that relating to the armistice with Bulgaria, signed in Moscow, October 28, 1944, is in *FR, 1944,* III, 300–481. Brief accounts may be found in Churchill, *Triumph and Tragedy,* 72–84; Woodward, *British Foreign Policy in the Second World War,* 294–97; Herbert Feis, *Churchill, Roosevelt and Stalin: The War They Waged and The Peace They Sought* (Princeton, 1957), 409–21. The latter is the best single volume on the diplomacy of the war.

agreed to a three-months' trial of the bilateral allocation, only
to have it extended to other nations and culminate in the
October 1944 Moscow disposition of authority.[17]

On these and many other questions "British policy was
based on the idea of cooperation with the Russians after the
war." [18] The extent to which the Western Allies would accede
to Russian demands in order to promote this cooperation was
a frequent source of contention between Roosevelt and
Churchill, both of whom sought at various times and in various
ways to restrain Soviet ambitions. In the case of the Balkans
the President's attempts to secure a greater Anglo-American
voice in affairs were frustrated by the Prime Minister, who
seemed so anxious to control events in Greece that he took the
initiative in turning other countries over to the Russians and
persuaded the United States to go along. While the Soviet
military presence may have made such an arrangement unavoidable, the Prime Minister's generous proposals weakened
subsequent claims for Anglo-American participation in the
administration of these states.

Much of the controversy over wartime diplomacy is fo-
cused on the fate of Poland. Russia, in spite of her formal
renunciation of the German treaties which had divided Poland,
had sought early in the war to gain British consent to a read-
justment of the Polish border, and the question emerged per-
iodically as the British followed the American lead in deferring
territorial settlements. When the Big Three met at Tehran in
November 1944, Churchill introduced the topic and expressed
the hope that an understanding could be reached on Polish
frontiers; that, as recorded in the minutes, "he personally had
no attachment to any specific frontier between Poland and the
Soviet Union; that he felt that the consideration of Soviet
security on their western frontier was a governing factor."

17. Correspondence is conveniently reproduced in Churchill, *Triumph and Tragedy,* 72–81.
18. Woodward, *British Foreign Policy in the Second World War,*
290. In this the Western Allies were not far apart on principle.

Then, to punctuate his remarks, "He said that, as far as he was concerned, he would like to see Poland moved westward in the same manner as soldiers at drill execute the drill 'left close' and illustrated his point with three matches representing the Soviet Union, Poland and Germany." [19] Later, at a luncheon meeting, when discussing the disposition of certain enemy-held territory, "The Prime Minister then said that it was important that the nations who would govern the world after the war, and who would be entrusted with the direction of the world after the war, should be satisfied and have no territorial or other ambitions. If that question could be settled in a manner agreeable to the great powers, he felt then that the world might indeed remain at peace." Elaborating on this theme, "He said that hungry nations and ambitious nations are dangerous, and he would like to see the leading nations of the world in the position of rich, happy men." [20] This open invitation for territorial aggrandizement probably gratified Stalin and disturbed the President, although both expressed concurrence with the sentiments. Explicitly contradicting publicly announced war aims, the Prime Minister's observation could serve only to aggravate the Russians' appetite and rigidify their claims.

Conversations on the specifics of Poland's postwar boundaries were opened indirectly by Stalin in reference to Germany, when he mentioned that Poland's western frontier should be on the Oder River.[21] As became apparent, this additional territory accruing to Poland at Germany's expense was to compensate for the Russian insistence on a restoration of the 1939–41 eastern border, and the arrangement seemed consistent with Churchill's graphic demonstration of Poland moving westward. The President had been confronted with this issue in March 1943 when Eden visited Washington, outlined

19. *FR, Conferences at Cairo and Tehran, 1943,* 512.
20. *Ibid.,* 568. For Churchill's paraphrase of these remarks see his *Closing the Ring,* 382.
21. See map, page 75.

the Soviet European demands, and confessed that in the postwar milieu "England would probably be too weak to face
Russia alone diplomatically." [22] At this time Roosevelt apparently indicated that Poland should be given East Prussia, but
whether he embraced the Curzon line as the boundary with
Russia is questionable.[23] The British at Tehran advocated this
solution, and thought it consistent with the Russian position.
Some map study revealed that except for a few details, including the disposition of Lvov, Churchill and Stalin reached
agreement on the geographical limits of the postwar Polish
state.[24] The Prime Minister, volunteering to present this proposal to the Polish government-in-exile in London, said that
"the Poles would be wise to take our advice," and that he
"was not prepared to make a big squawk about Lvov." [25] As
it turned out, the London Poles did make a big squawk about
the entire eastern boundary question, made no headway with
an exasperated Churchill, and appealed to Roosevelt to cham-
pion their cause for a restoration of what they considered their
legitimate frontiers.

During these deliberations at Tehran on the Polish boundaries, the President remained largely silent, interposing an
occasional question and suggesting only that diplomatic relations be resumed between the Polish government-in-exile and

22. *FR, 1943*, III, 13.
23. For memoranda of these conversations see *ibid.*, 13–17, 22–24.
Woodward implies that Roosevelt did endorse the Curzon Line. *British
Foreign Policy in World War II*, 439. For an absorbing account of the
President's thorough preparation for his "summit conferences," see Henry
Field, "How F.D.R. Did His Homework," *Saturday Review*, July 8,
1961, 8–10, 46.
24. *FR, Conferences at Cairo and Tehran, 1943*, 598–602, 604;
Franklin, "Yalta Viewed from Tehran," 257–58; Churchill, *Closing the
Ring*, 394–97; Woodward, *British Foreign Policy in World War II*, 253–
54. The complexities of this issue are illustrated by one authority's
statement that "It is simply not clear where Poland begins and ends."
Henry L. Robert, "The Diplomacy of Colonel Beck," in Gordon A.
Craig and Felix Gilbert, eds., *The Diplomats, 1919–1939* (Princeton,
1953), 583.
25. Churchill, *Closing the Ring*, 397.

the Kremlin, relations having been severed by the Russian government over actions by the London Poles in regard to German allegations that Russian troops had massacred thousands of Polish officers. Speaking privately with Stalin, the President explained that there were six or seven million voters of Polish extraction in the United States and he might feel it necessary to run for re-election in 1944. Any position he took at this time on the future of Poland could be embarrassing and prove harmful to his chances. Stalin indicated his understanding and seemed unperturbed by the minimal American participation in the question or the absence of concurrence in the Anglo-Russian solution.[26] Perhaps he accepted the President's explanation, perhaps he was confident that the United States would support the British position, and perhaps he did not care what his allies thought because Russian troops were gaining possession of the area and would have the power of decision.

Regardless of Stalin's motives, those of the President were probably more complex than he admitted. His minimal participation in the boundary issue must be viewed in the context of his repeated reluctance to resolve European territorial adjustments while the war was still undecided. The military situation in November 1943 placed the Western Allies in a distinctly weak bargaining position, for the offensive in Italy was bogged down, the Russians were driving back the Germans on the Eastern front, and a firm commitment for a late-spring 1944 cross-channel invasion was made belatedly at Tehran. Clearly the circumstances were not propitious for a confrontation with the Russians over matters which they regarded as of primary interest. Consistent with his predilection for postponing settlements, Roosevelt was to conserve his efforts for Yalta, when he not only was relieved of apprehensions over re-election but when Anglo-American forces were making a significantly greater contribution to the defeat of Germany.

26. *FR, Conferences at Cairo and Tehran, 1943,* 594.

Whether the Prime Minister's introduction of the Polish question at Tehran was premature is debatable, but he certainly must accept primary responsibility for acceptance of the Russian demands. Furthermore, it is unlikely that the President's intercession at this time would have affected the outcome, for reasons already indicated and because he would have found himself in a minority at odds with his British colleague and the Soviet leader. Under the circumstances delay seemed the best tactic in the hope that prospects for concessions might improve.[27] Besides, at this stage in the war an altercation over boundaries could upset the precarious military collaboration that offered the best, if not the only, means of defeating Hitler.

One of the more eventful and long-drawn-out-controversies between Roosevelt and Churchill concerned the occupation of Germany after her defeat, specifically which area would be controlled by each of the victorious powers. At the Moscow Conference in October 1943, Hull submitted a proposal entitled "The Treatment of Germany," which "recommended that the occupation of Germany be effected by contingents of British, Soviet and American forces," but did not indicate whether this should be joint or separate by zones.[28] The following month, Roosevelt, en route to conferences at Cairo and Tehran on board the battleship U.S.S. *Iowa,* discussed with the Joint Chiefs of Staff a British proposal for an assault on Western Europe which specified that the British would occupy Northwestern Germany and the United States the portion south of the Moselle River. Objecting on the grounds that France was Britain's "baby" and that the United States could best use the northern German ports, the President advocated a reversal of the British plan with the American zone encompassing Berlin and the Soviet Union controlling the area to the east.

27. Churchill writes that at the end of the discussion at Tehran on the Polish question, "Turning to Marshal Stalin, I added that I did not think we were very far apart in principle." *Closing the Ring,* 397.
28. *FR, Conferences at Cairo and Tehran, 1943,* 184.

"The United States should have Berlin," the President stated, and, he observed, "There would definitely be a race for Berlin." [29] Later the entire matter became enmeshed with the question over the dismemberment of Germany and the broader problems of administering Europe after hostilities ended, so a European Advisory Commission was established in London to study and make recommendations on these problems.

Composed of representatives from the United States, Great Britain, and the Soviet Union, the Commission discovered that occupation zones constituted one of its more vexing tasks. Before the American representative, Ambassador John G. Winant, had received any instructions from his government on the question, the British presented a detailed proposal which was quickly approved by the Russians. Based on the plan incorporated in the earlier military document, it assigned the Northwest zone to Britain, the Southern to the United States, and the Eastern to the Soviet Union. The Berlin area, some 110 miles inside the Soviet zone, was to be a "separate Combined Zone occupied by selected troops representing, in due proportions, all the Allied forces of occupation. The principal role of this mixed force would be to support the authority of any Allied Military Government, the Control Commission and other Allied bodies and also to ensure the maintenance of order in the Capital." [30] Reacting adversely to this proposal, the President directed that Winant hold out for American occupation of the Northern zone. [31] Oddly enough, he made no objections to the incorporation of Berlin within the Soviet zone, which not long before he had opposed. Perhaps Roosevelt was reluctant to enter into a controversy with the Prime

29. *Ibid.,* 253–55. Roosevelt believed that revolution in France was likely after liberation. De Gaulle and his followers would be striving to eliminate the Vichy government, and the resistance movement, heavily infused with communists, might seek its own solution. The President simply did not want to become involved in this internecine struggle.

30. *FR, 1944,* I, 152.

31. *Ibid.,* 184.

Minister over an issue which he felt was of primary interest to the British and only secondarily of concern to the United States, but evidently he placed the geographical location of the occupation zone ahead of his original desire to incorporate Berlin in the American area. Possibly he became reconciled to the fact that Russian troops would probably reach Berlin first, and, since he was faced with Anglo-Soviet agreement on tripartite control of the German capital, his views could not prevail. The juxtaposition of American and British zones was a different proposition, for this constituted a bilateral rather than a multilateral arrangement.

For seven months the President and the Prime Minister held their positions and carried on the dispute in direct communications and through their harassed subordinates. The American case was based on the supply factor in regard to the north German ports, the desire to avoid "the postwar burden of reconstituting France, Italy, and the Balkans," and unspecified "political considerations." [32] The British case rested on the imperatives of military operations which projected the deployment of troops in the invasion of Western Europe and the difficulty of effecting a transfer after surrender. Eventually the President did bow to Churchill's adamancy, probably because he felt the issue not sufficiently important to create a break and because he was primarily concerned with maintaining Anglo-American unity in the face of growing Soviet intractability. Roosevelt was looking forward to a peace that would be enforced by the victorious major powers. Only by continued collaboration with Britain and Russia could this objective be achieved, and he was able to reconcile himself to losing some of the short-range goals in order to secure support for his long-range project.

The President may have had reasons for wanting to occupy northwest Germany that he did not mention, but his persistence is in surprising contrast to the ease with which he relinquished Berlin. Apparently foresighted in perceiving the

32. *Ibid.*

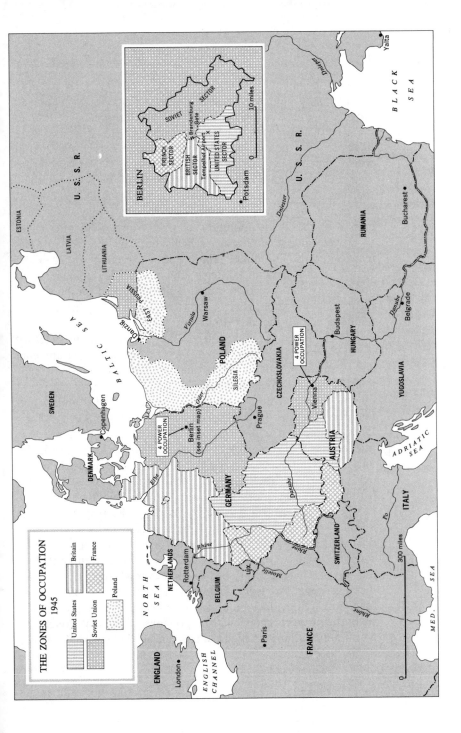

THE ZONES OF OCCUPATION
1945

United States
Soviet Union
Britain
France
Poland

BERLIN

SOVIET SECTOR
FRENCH SECTOR
BRITISH SECTOR
Brandenburg Gate
Tempelhof Airport
UNITED STATES SECTOR
0   10 miles
Potsdam

ENGLAND
London
ENGLISH CHANNEL
NORTH SEA
Paris
FRANCE
Rotterdam
NETHERLANDS
BELGIUM
Lux.
Moselle
Rhine
SWITZERLAND
0   300 miles
MED. SEA
ITALY
Po
Rhône
Danube
AUSTRIA
4 POWER OCCUPATION
Vienna
GERMANY
Elbe
Berlin
(see inset map)
4 POWER OCCUPATION
Prague
CZECHOSLOVAKIA
HUNGARY
Budapest
Danube
YUGOSLAVIA
Belgrade
ADRIATIC SEA
DENMARK
Copenhagen
BALTIC SEA
SWEDEN
DANZIG
EAST PRUSSIA
SILESIA
Oder
Vistula
Warsaw
POLAND
LITHUANIA
LATVIA
ESTONIA
U. S. S. R.
Dniester
Dniester
Bucharest
RUMANIA
Danube
BLACK SEA
Yalta
Pruth

strategic advantage of occupying the capital, he reluctantly accepted the military realities dictated by the long-delayed Anglo-American incursion into Western Europe. Acceding to the British peripheral approach meant that the Russians were likely to take possession of much of eastern Germany, from which they could not easily be dislodged. They, too, were aware of the significance of the capture of Berlin, and they, too, had read Clausewitz, who designated a nation's capital as the center of gravity in war. The President may well have embraced the British solution as a less distasteful alternative to Soviet control of the city which could be the key to Germany's future. The direct relationship is apparent between the British and American strategic differences, the influence that military dispositions, current and anticipated, had on the assignment of occupation zones, and the implications for postwar relations among the victorious powers.

When the Soviet blockade of Berlin occurred in 1948–49 the question was raised about any agreement guaranteeing access to the jointly occupied and administered German capital. On a visit to Washington in May 1944 Winant had brought up the matter with the War Department, for he understood that the Russians would be amenable. But the Civil Affairs Division opposed a discussion of the subject, contending that at the time it was not clear which routes would be available. Subsequent attempts by Winant to inject the issue into the deliberations of the European Advisory Commission were frustrated by the War Department, which held that it was a purely military concern to be resolved by the respective commanders. The American Joint Chiefs of Staff did propose freedom of transit across all zones of occupation, a proposal which was approved by the British Chiefs of Staff and submitted to the Soviet General Staff but never acknowledged. Eventually the European Advisory Commission provided explicitly for road, rail, water, and air access to Vienna and by implication to Berlin in accordance with a previous settlement concluded by military authorities of the three nations. While Anglo-American rights of transit to and from the German capital may not have been spelled out in a formal document, they were quite well established in the minds of some of the negotiators at the time.[33]

The Polish issue, which had simmered intermittently since Tehran, threatened to boil over at Yalta when the Big Three met in February 1945. No longer did military affairs dominate the agenda, for Allied forces were driving into the heart of Germany, and surrender was merely a matter of time. At Yalta the leaders of the victorious nations gathered to divide the spoils and resolve the thorny political questions that accompanied conquest. Here was the moment of truth, when the noble phrases of the Atlantic Charter and the Declaration of the United Nations would find their greatest challenge as the aspirations of the victors took concrete form.

Prior to the meeting the United States publicly reiterated its "consistently held policy" that "questions relating to boundaries should be left in abeyance until the termination of hostilities," with exceptions permitted if "settled by friendly conference and agreement." [34] Poland's boundaries, which affected those of other nations, were to be an exception, and this problem was compounded by the question of which government was to exercise control in the liberated country. Since relations between the London exiles and the Kremlin had

33. See William M. Franklin, "Zonal Boundaries and Access to Berlin," *World Politics*, XVI (1963), 1–31; Philip E. Mosely, "The Occupation of Germany: New Light on How the Zones Were Drawn," in *The Kremlin and World Politics: Studies in Soviet Policy and Action* (New York, 1960), 154–88, originally published in *Foreign Affairs*, XXVIII (1950), 580–604. Eisenhower's political adviser on Germany, Robert Murphy, says he raised the topic with Winant, who refused to revive it with the Commission. "In Winant's opinion, if we now belatedly raised the access question, this might upset the hard-won draft agreement [of September 12, 1944] and make further settlements impossible. Winant argued that our right of free access to Berlin was implicit in our right to be there." Robert Murphy, *Diplomat Among Warriors* (Garden City, N.Y., 1964), 231–32.

34. Department of State Press Release, December 18, 1944, *FR, Conferences at Malta and Yalta, 1945*, 218–19.

deteriorated, a new body had been formed in Lublin with Russian encouragement. Vigorous efforts by Roosevelt and Churchill to prevent a formal recognition of the Lublin Committee by the Soviet Government prior to the summit meeting were unsuccessful, and the two Western leaders found themselves faced with another accomplished fact. Stalin justified his action on the grounds of primary concern, his nation having borne "the main brunt of the battle for the liberation of Poland" and being rightfully anxious to provide for its own security.[35] Numerous discussions resulted in a compromise whereby a new provisional government was to be formed consisting of representatives from the London and Lublin (now located in Warsaw) groups. This interim body, to be recognized by the three Great Powers, was pledged to "the holding of free and unfettered elections as soon as possible on the basis of universal suffrage and secret ballot." [36] The task of composing this new government was assigned to a commission made up of the British and American ambassadors to the Soviet Union and Soviet Foreign Minister Molotov, with the latter frustrating what his two colleagues considered the letter and spirit of the Yalta accord. Yet, since the Russians occupied the country, there was little that the Western Allies could do other than protest, so the new provisional government and the elections were at the mercy of and carried out the will of the liberators.

As for boundaries, that in the east was to conform to the Curzon line with slight adjustments in favor of Poland. Roosevelt, with Churchill's support, made a strong plea for the inclusion of Lvov and some oil fields, but Stalin would not budge. The western boundary, Churchill urged, should go as far as the Oder, but he protested its extension to the western Niesse. Here he was hoist on the petard he had raised at Tehran, and final details on boundaries were left to be decided by a future conference after consultation with the Polish govern-

35. *Ibid.,* 221–23.
36. *Ibid.,* 973.

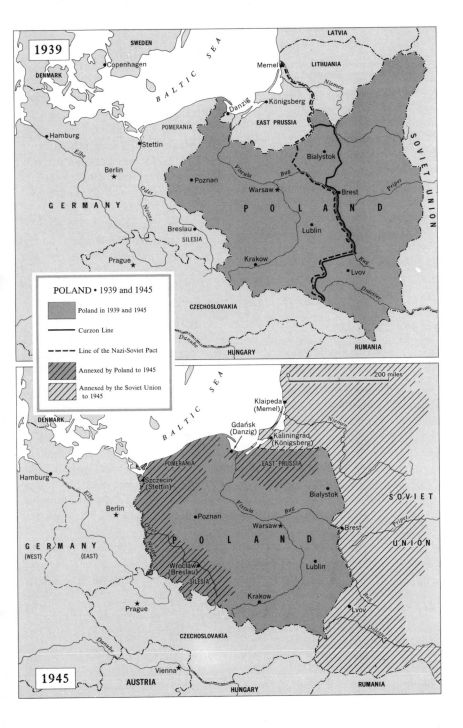

1939

SWEDEN

DENMARK

Copenhagen

BALTIC SEA

LATVIA

Memel

LITHUANIA

Niemen

Danzig

Königsberg

EAST PRUSSIA

Hamburg

POMERANIA

Stettin

Elbe

Berlin

★

Bialystok

Poznan

Vistula

Bug

G E R M A N Y

Oder

Warsaw ★

Pripet

P O L A N D

Neisse

S O V I E T

U N I O N

Breslau

Lublin

SILESIA

Brest

Prague ★

Krakow

Bug

Lvov

Dniester

POLAND • 1939 and 1945

Poland in 1939 and 1945

Curzon Line

Line of the Nazi-Soviet Pact

Annexed by Poland to 1945

Annexed by the Soviet Union
to 1945

CZECHOSLOVAKIA

Danube

HUNGARY

RUMANIA

0   200 miles

BALTIC SEA

Klaipeda
(Memel)

DENMARK

Gdańsk
(Danzig)

Kaliningrad
(Königsberg)

Niemen

Hamburg

POMERANIA

EAST PRUSSIA

Szczecin
(Stettin)

Bialystok

S O V I E T

Berlin

★

Vistula

Bug

Poznan

G E R M A N Y

Oder

Warsaw ★

Pripet

(WEST)   (EAST)

Neisse

P O L A N D

Brest

U N I O N

Wrocław
(Breslau)

Lublin

SILESIA

Prague ★

Krakow

Bug

Lvov

Dniester

CZECHOSLOVAKIA

Danube

1945

Vienna ★

AUSTRIA

HUNGARY

RUMANIA

ment.[37] The issue was probably postponed not only out of deference to the Poles or in order to avoid a substantive altercation, but also because the President mentioned that specific boundaries required Senate approval. Familiar with the treaty clause in the Constitution, Roosevelt often interpreted it in the light of the circumstances. The distinction between a treaty and an executive agreement at times seemed not to bother him, especially when allocating territories which formed a part of the defeated nations.

Aside from the general terms for the liberation of peoples contained in the Atlantic Charter and the Declaration of the United Nations, little had been said publicly about postwar territorial adjustments until the Cairo Conference in late 1943 when Roosevelt, Churchill, and President Chiang Kai-shek of China decided the fate of the Japanese Empire. As stated in the joint press release of December 1, 1943:

It is their purpose that Japan shall be stripped of all the islands in the Pacific which she has seized or occupied since the beginning of the first World War in 1914, and that all the territories Japan has stolen from the Chinese, such as Manchuria, Formosa, and the Pescadores, shall be restored to the Republic of China. Japan will also be expelled from all other territories which she has taken by violence and greed. The aforesaid three great powers, mindful of the enslavement of the people of Korea, are determined that in due course Korea shall become free and independent.[38]

Thus the President committed his nation to a most specific and far-reaching allocation of territory in the Far East, and this announcement brought home to the Japanese the consequences of defeat in a far more meaningful way than did the ominous ring of "unconditional surrender."

At Yalta the Far East appeared on the agenda in regard to

---

37. In November 1970, the West German and Polish governments signed a treaty acknowledging the line formed by the Oder and Neisse rivers as Poland's western frontier. Specifying a temporary rather than a final or definitive solution of the boundary, this agreement had not been ratified by the two governments at date of this writing.

38. *FR, Conferences at Cairo and Tehran, 1943,* 448–49.

the price Russia demanded for her entry into the war against Japan, an event to take place some two or three months after Germany's collapse. Stalin had made the commitment at the Foreign Ministers' Conference at Moscow in October 1943, and he reaffirmed his intention a month later at Tehran. Now, at Yalta, with the European conflict nearing its end, the time had come to exact compensation. In fixing his demands, Stalin insisted that he must explain to his people why they were entering a new war, namely, in order to gain certain advantages, and that these advantages must be in some degree proportionate to the anticipated sacrifices. The President, who conducted these negotiations with the Soviet leader, was under heavy pressure from his military advisers to gain the assistance of this powerful ally whose contribution promised to reduce considerably the predicted huge American casualties and shorten the Pacific conflict.[39] Stalin carefully enumerated his conditions, some of which Roosevelt vainly attempted to alter. The final agreement signed by the three leaders included assurance of the autonomy of Outer Mongolia; the restoration of the "former rights of Russia" relinquished as a result of the Russo-Japanese War, which as stipulated in the Yalta document included the return of the southern part of Sakhalin; the internationalization of the port of Dairen; the lease of Port Arthur as a naval base; the operation by a joint Soviet-Chinese Company of the Chinese-Eastern Railroad and the South-Manchurian Railroad; and the outright award of the Kuril Islands to the Soviet Union. Since the signatories realized that some of the items would require the concurrence of Generalissimo Chiang Kai-shek, the document pledged Roosevelt to secure this concurrence but added that "these claims of the Soviet Union shall be unquestionably fulfilled after Japan has been defeated." [40]

To deprive an enemy of territory after conquest was con-

---

39. Plans for Japan's defeat and implications of the Atomic bomb are discussed on pp. 89 ff.
40. *FR, Conferences at Malta and Yalta, 1945*, 984.

ventional practice, but to inflict similar penalties on an ally without his participation in the decision was a departure from precedent and from the principles agreed to by the United Nations. Of course Russia had historical claims to much of what she demanded, some of which had been extorted from China half a century earlier. But previous ownership or control, while a dominant factor in validating territorial claims, could not be the sole criterion. Such logic could lead, as Roosevelt observed at one point, to Churchill demanding that the United States be returned to Great Britain. Still, it seemed clear that Russia could take from China what she wanted, and it was desirable to gain support for the Chiang government rather than antagonize the Soviet neighbor. Essentially, it is doubtful that American anxiety for Soviet participation in the war against Japan was primarily responsible for the concessions made at China's expense. Of greater significance may have been the President's realization that Stalin's method of gaining these "former rights" and insuring the separation of Outer Mongolia might have been fatal to the Kuomintang government of Chiang Kai-shek and China's future role as a power in the Far East.

Roosevelt's predilection for including China among the great powers amounted, in Churchill's opinion, to a virtual obsession. The Prime Minister had little more than contempt for this sprawling disorganized nation and the Chiang government, which had failed to provide unity or wage war effectively against Japan. Moreover, the anti-imperialist tendencies of the Kuomintang government jeopardized British interests in China, held dire implications for the key British outpost of Hong Kong, and threatened the entire British position in Asia. Roosevelt, in promoting China as an equal of the Big Three in numerous wartime pronouncements if not always in consultation, used many arguments to support his stand. During conversations with Eden in March 1943 he contended that China could help "police" the Far East after Japan had been destroyed, and that "China, in any serious conflict of policy with Russia, would undoubtedly line up on our side." Later, issuing instructions to Hull before the Moscow Conference, he wrote, "China is too important a factor, both now and in the future, both because of herself and because of her influence over British India, to be alienated." At Tehran Roosevelt noted that it was better to have a country of four hundred million people "as friends rather than as a potential source of trouble." Also aware that China had been given relatively little military assistance, he may have felt that other concessions were warranted to compensate for inequities in the allocation of American resources. While all of these justifications had some validity, it is likely that his predominant motive was his conviction that, with Japanese power destroyed, some means had to be found to counter Soviet influence in the Far East. There was no other nation to replace Japan in maintaining some semblance of a balance of power in that part of the world, and Chiang's government offered the only viable alternative to Communist domination. Whether the Chinese Communists were merely agrarian reformers—as believed by some of the President's advisers—was not a decisive factor. Prosecution of the war against Japan, preserving peace through international cooperation, and stability in Asia could best be assured by China's membership in the Big Four coterie that was to control the world.

The Yalta Conference also provided final agreement on the terms for the surrender of Germany. For months the European Advisory Commission had worked on particulars, clearing many perplexing details with the respective governments. At Yalta Stalin questioned the unconditional surrender formula in regard to specifics. What were the Allies to do, he asked, if Hitler offered to surrender unconditionally, or if he were overthrown by a group which accepted these terms? Churchill responded in the strongest language that negotiations with Hitler or Himmler were inconceivable, and that if some new group made overtures the Allies would consult as to what should be done. The Germans should not be informed of Allied plans for the future of Germany, the Prime Minister added, and they should be compelled to submit to the undeclared will of the victors. Stalin, insisting that the Germans should have some warning of what was in store for them, thought that at least they should be informed of the intention to dismember the nation and be prepared to accept this drastic action. The President agreed with Stalin in spite of Churchill's apprehension that this knowledge might increase resistance, and finally the three leaders decided to incorporate a statement of intention to dismember Germany in the surrender terms.[41]

The communiqué issued at the conclusion of the conference alerted everyone to Germany's fate. Although dismemberment was not mentioned, unconditional surrender was reaffirmed, and machinery for the occupation and control of Germany was indicated. Enumerated were the steps to be taken to destroy Germany's military capability, eradicate Nazism, punish war criminals, and exact reparations in kind for damage inflicted.[42] While many details included in the surrender document were missing, the communiqué left no doubt in anyone's mind that the victors were determined to impose a harsh and uncompromising peace.

Yalta marked the apogee of wartime diplomacy. Major problems of postwar reconstruction were resolved, if not to everyone's satisfaction; and essentially each of the leaders achieved his objectives. Critics of the President have labeled his performance a "betrayal," alleging a sell-out to communism which has been attributed variously to his ill health, his Marxist sympathies, his stubborn rejection of the advice given him by his subordinates or by Churchill, his preoccupation with world organization, or his obsession with the purely military dimensions of the war. In retrospect, however, it appears that Roosevelt accomplished as much as could be reasonably expected, although not as much as he had hoped. The solution for a Polish government was not entirely satisfactory, but it

41. *Ibid.,* 612–16, 624, 627–28.
42. *Ibid.,* 970–71.

represented a modest compromise by the Russians, whose military liberation of the country placed them in an unassailable position. The greatest discord was to arise from the later interpretation and implementation of the agreement on the provisional government and the free elections. The main source of friction in regard to Germany arose over the amount of reparations, which was put in the hands of a commission to meet in Moscow. Stalin consented to French participation in the German Control Commission and to France's being given an occupation zone carved from the territory allocated to the United States and Great Britain. More importantly, he accepted what was probably the most vital of Roosevelt's war aims, namely, a world organization of nations to preserve peace. Soviet adherence to this proposal and approval of the basic operational procedures was a notable achievement, for the President was determined to curtail the international anarchy which permitted, if it did not encourage, aggression.[43]

Under this protective umbrella of collective security nations were to work out their problems without resort to war, and aspiring "criminals" would be chastened by the overwhelming military superiority of the great powers. Within the context of this pacific world the peoples could strive for political, social, and economic reform to inaugurate a new era in the history of mankind. An impossible dream perhaps, but this is what Roosevelt believed America was fighting for, and in his pragmatic way he subordinated other considerations to its realization. Of course it is seldom possible to effect a negotiated agreement in which all the advantages accrue to one side, and Roosevelt knew that compromise was one of the arts of diplomacy. But even assuming that world organization was not important, what else could have been accomplished? Neither Roosevelt nor Churchill could thwart basic Soviet ambi-

43. The assertion that Roosevelt at Yalta was in such poor health that his mental faculties were impaired has been denied by the President's personal physician at the time, Dr. Howard G. Bruenn, in an article in the April 1970 issue of *Annals of Internal Medicine.*

tions in Europe and the Far East.

In the weeks following the Yalta Conference and as British, American, and Russian representatives argued over the meaning of certain provisions of the Yalta accords, the most serious altercation among the Allies developed over alleged surreptitious contacts with German authorities. Stalin's blunt accusation of American complicity brought an angry denial from the President, and the incident threatened to upset the entire framework of Allied unity. Meanwhile German forces were being driven back on all fronts and speculation mounted over who would capture Berlin. Roosevelt's earlier prophecy that there would be a race for Berlin may have been remembered by some, but evidently the President was no longer interested in this particular competition. He had raised the issue at a time when he envisioned the German capital being incorporated in the American occupation zone. Since then the Prime Minister's views on the subject had prevailed, and Berlin was located well inside the Soviet zone to be administered under joint supervision. At this point troop movements no longer had any political significance, and Roosevelt was willing to leave these military judgments to the professionals. The decision to stop the American advance at the Elbe River was made by General Eisenhower in his capacity as Supreme Allied Commander. Based on purely military considerations determined by the most effective allocation of resources to destroy the enemy defenders and save American lives, the decision had no effect on the future of Germany, the influence of the Western Allies in her affairs, or the Soviet role in Berlin.[44]

Whether this action had a bearing on the timing of the German surrender is another matter. Assuming that the American forces could have reached Berlin before the Russians, which is questionable, would there have been such a desperate,

44. See Stephen E. Ambrose, *Eisenhower and Berlin, 1945: The Decision to Halt at the Elbe* (New York, 1967); and Forrest C. Pogue, "The Decision to Halt at the Elbe (1945)," in Kent Roberts Greenfield, ed., *Command Decisions* (New York, 1959), 374–87.

last-ditch defense of the capital? As defeat appeared inevitable, the Germans, fearful of the Russians, sought capitulation to the Western Allies, in the firm conviction that treatment would be more humane. If the American troops had approached Berlin, would Hitler have been able to maintain his authority? Would he have been replaced earlier by leaders so anxious to preserve the capital that they would have been willing to surrender, knowing that Berlin would first be occupied by American forces? No other advantage could be gained by an American thrust, and there was no apparent justification for the gamble under the circumstances.

5

Final Victory

AS THE ALLIED troops drove into Germany, some British and American members of Eisenhower's staff, including his political adviser for Germany, Robert Murphy, attempted to persuade Washington to consent to an overture for peace based on "conditional unconditional surrender" terms. Emphatically rejecting this suggestion, Secretary of State Edward R. Stettinius, Jr., reaffirmed the consistently maintained policy which was to apply "without exception, to all Germans, individually and collectively, in all respects, including the sense in which the German people may be considered as individual human beings." [1] This message, dispatched two days before the President's death on April 12, 1945, probably represented his final thoughts on the subject. More than ever he seemed convinced of the correctness of his position, and he had no intention of wavering when victory was at hand.

Nor did Roosevelt's successor, Harry S. Truman, weaken in the determination to insist on total German submission. When an offer to surrender on the Western front was made through a Swedish emissary by Heinrich Himmler, who claimed to be head of the German government because of Hitler's illness, both Truman and Churchill, in a trans-Atlantic telephone conversation, agreed that they should accept nothing less than unconditional surrender to the three governments on

1. *FR, 1945,* III, 751. A survey of public opinion conducted in the spring of 1945 revealed 81 percent of the respondents favorable to the doctrine. *Opinion News,* March 20, 1945, 2.

all fronts simultaneously.[2] The news of Hitler's death on May 1 enheartened the Allies by removing a major obstacle to peace. Some two years earlier the American ambassador to Spain had reported that the Argentine ambassador told him of a conversation with the Rumanian minister, who said that Jon Antonescu, Rumanian chief of state, recently had talked with the Führer. Germany could not win the war, Hitler acknowledged, but it did constitute the last bulwark against communism in Europe. He was willing to restore most conquered territories with the understanding that "peace would be guaranteed by [a] united force of Germans and Anglo-Saxons." Hitler, of course, would have to remain in power.[3] As the situation deteriorated the Führer began to vacillate, and in August 1944 he declared that if the German people were to be overcome, "then it had been too weak to face the test of history, and was fit only for destruction." In April 1945, apprised of secret peace overtures by subordinates, he told advisers that continued fighting was useless and negotiations were desirable, although he took no initiative and issued no instructions. When chaos in Nazi circles reached a crescendo, Hitler committed suicide, and his appointed successor, Grand Admiral Karl Doenitz, frantically strove to capitulate only to the Western Allies. Hoping to save as many Germans as possible from the Soviets, his efforts were thwarted by the Supreme Commander's insistence that the surrender be effected on all fronts simultaneously. Faced with a hopeless military situation and the firm unity of his foes, the new Reich president reluctantly ordered the acceptance of Allied terms.[4]

2. Transcript of telephone conversation, April 25, 1945, *FR, 1945,* III, 762–67.
3. *FR, 1943,* I, 485–86. See *ibid.,* 484–512, for "peace-feeler approaches from the Axis nations."
4. *FR, 1945,* III, 777. The confused state of affairs in Germany during this period is portrayed in H. R. Trevor-Roper, *The Last Days of Hitler* (New York, 1947), and William L. Shirer, *The Rise and Fall of the Third Reich: A History of Nazi Germany* (New York, 1960), 1107–40.

The surrender, finally effected at Eisenhower's headquarters on May 7, 1945, was "ratified" the following day in Berlin. Evidently the first document signed by the representatives had been hastily drawn up locally, and a second ceremony was necessary using the terms prepared by the European Advisory Commission and approved by the respective governments.[5] The Supreme Allied Commander was now able to report that his assigned mission had been completed.[6]

Significantly, the surrender was effected by the German High Command as authorized by Admiral Doenitz, with Eisenhower acting as the agent of the three allies. The details of subjugation were spelled out in the Allied Declaration of June 5, which simply decreed the victor's absolute control of Germany.

Ever since the Casablanca announcement a distinction had been drawn between a military surrender and a political surrender. The former could be accomplished by the appropriate military authority in a local situation on a particular front, although the magnitude of the operation and the form of the negotiation were not always clear, as Roosevelt had learned to his chagrin. A singular feature of the unconditional surrender formula was that it encompassed both the military and political dimensions of capitulation, and the Big Three adhered to this comprehensive application to Germany. General Eisenhower and Admiral King were among the military leaders who came to doubt the wisdom of this policy, contending that it stiffened resistance and made their job, namely, defeating the enemy forces, more difficult, an attitude that reflected a primary concern with what was their basic responsibility. The political leaders were compelled to look beyond the battles, which served as an indispensable means to achieve the purposes of the war. This fundamental dichotomy between the

5. A detailed account of the surrender is in Forrest C. Pogue, *The Supreme Command* (Washington, D.C., 1954), 475–94.
6. Chandler and Ambrose, *The Papers of Dwight D. Eisenhower,* IV, 2696.

statesmen and their military advisers was seldom more obvious than when manifested in their difference over the unconditional surrender policy. But there is no evidence that the Joint Chiefs of Staff or the commanders in the field ever confronted the President directly on this issue. Pressure for modification came from other sources within or outside the structure of government.

Fortunately Roosevelt was spared excessive division in his own camp on this matter, but he encountered a great deal of opposition from his foreign associates. Coalition warfare was sufficiently complex, and coalition diplomacy held the prospect of more ominous pitfalls. The absence of restrictions on the actions of the victors, formally accepted by the vanquished, provided a framework within which the machinery for the occupation and control of Germany could be formulated. If there had been a desire on the part of any one of the Allies to negotiate for conditions with whatever German government appeared to exist, the dispute might well have created the split between the Anglo-American and Soviet authorities which the enemy sought to promote. The President's formula helped prevent such a disastrous outcome at this crucial stage in bringing the war to an end.

The most vigorous indictment of the unconditional surrender policy comes from those who contend that it prolonged the war by discouraging certain opposition groups in Germany from seizing the reins of government and suing for a negotiated peace. This harsh dictum, it is alleged, left the Germans no alternative to continued resistance, produced unnecessary casualties and devastation, and opened much of Europe to Communist domination.[7] The validity of this contention rests on (1) the prospects of these groups gaining power and (2) whether the terms upon which they would have insisted would have been acceptable to any or all of the Allies. Hitler

7. The fullest critique is Anne Armstrong, *Unconditional Surrender: The Impact of the Casablanca Policy Upon World War II* (New Brunswick, N.J., 1961).

could be removed only if the army cooperated, and as the July 20, 1944, assassination attempt revealed, the officers would have taken over the government. Their motives were simple: to salvage whatever they could from a war they believed was lost. They wanted to prevent the complete destruction of the army and the nation, to extricate Germany from a hopeless situation, and to preserve its basic structure. Only through a compromise peace could this be achieved, a compromise peace with the Western Allies at the expense of the Soviet Union.[8] Essentially, the new masters would have demanded acquiescence to Germany's 1939 borders, no occupation of the country, no interference in internal affairs, no denazification, no punishment of war criminals, and no demilitarization. So the Western Allies would have had to accept a virtual pact against Russia and allow Germany to retain all of the ingredients for mischief except one: the Führer.

It is inconceivable that any of the Allied war leaders would have seriously considered such a proposal. Both Churchill and Roosevelt were firmly convinced that postwar cooperation with the Soviet Union was essential to maintain peace in the world, and both were equally convinced that Germany's potential for aggression must be destroyed. Too much time and effort had been expended, too much suffering had been endured, to even contemplate such a deal. Moreover, news that such an idea was being entertained would have split the coalition and created a violent public reaction in the United States and Great Britain that would have crippled the war effort and shaken confidence in the governments. To change opinion in a democracy on highly charged issues of war and peace is not a simple process, and the public mood was not conducive to a magnanimous treatment of this murderous enemy.

Some elements of the German underground resistance envisioned a negotiated settlement that would concede some of the Allied demands, but these factions had no chance of over-

8. As acknowledged *ibid.,* 254.

throwing Hitler, because they could not secure the support of the military. Nothing that the Allies could do or say would have helped their cause, and any attempt to do so probably would have strengthened the Nazi hold. For these groups to have fomented a civil war would have defeated their purpose, for that would have made the Allied conquest easier. The unconditional surrender policy may have provided grist for the Nazi propaganda mill. But it was not responsible for the failure to establish a new German government, and it did not eliminate the opportunity for peace overtures. Holding out the prospect of more favorable terms might have had a slight psychological impact on some Germans who, unfortunately, were in no position to do anything about it. The ruthless extermination of those suspected of complicity in the assassination plot revealed the fate of any who tried to oppose the government.[9]

Germany was the second of the three nations included in the original Casablanca declaration to succumb to the Allies. At Yalta Roosevelt sealed a compact with Stalin for Soviet participation in the war against Japan which American planners estimated could last another eighteen months. Notified shortly before the Yalta Conference that nuclear bombs would be available by summer, the President and his advisers evidently preferred to rely on a potential but proven ally rather than relying solely on a potential untested weapon. General Leslie R. Groves, head of the Manhattan District Project, advised in December 1944 that the first of the most powerful type of bomb, estimated to produce an explosion equivalent to

9. For different conclusions see *ibid.;* Hans Rothfels, *The German Opposition to Hitler: An Appraisal,* translated by Lawrence Wilson (revised edition, Chicago, 1962); Mary Alice Gallin, *German Resistance to Hitler: Ethical and Religious Factors* (Washington, D.C., 1961). More consistent with this author's views is *The German Resistance to Hitler: Resistance Thinking on Foreign Policy,* by Hermann Graml; *Social Views and Constitutional Plans of the Resistance,* by Hans Mommsen; *Resistance in the Labour Movement,* by Hans-Joachim Reichardt; *Political and Moral Motives Behind the Resistance,* by Ernst Wolf, Introduction by F. L. Carsten (Berkeley and Los Angeles, 1970).

ten thousand tons of TNT, would be ready around the first of August, with a second to be available by the end of the year. Another type, with a force equal to some five hundred tons of TNT, was expected by the end of July, and Groves explained that it had been delayed "by scientific difficulties which we have not as yet been able to solve." [10] When the Big Three met at Yalta the American authorities had no assurance that the bomb would detonate, that it could be delivered as an effective instrument of war, or that it would be available in sufficient quantity to be decisive. That the President contemplated its employment is revealed by his authorizing steps to prepare for this eventuality.[11] Nevertheless, the Russian army was a proven commodity, and it offered a more reliable solution to the problem of a lengthy war and additional casualties.

Truman inherited the contract made by his predecessor, although phenomenal American advances in the Pacific and the successful test of the atomic bomb raised doubts regarding the necessity or the desirability of Russian involvement in the Asian conflict. In his formal announcement on May 8, 1945, of the German capitulation, the new President warned Japan that the United States would now concentrate its efforts in the Pacific and "not cease until the Japanese military and naval forces lay down their arms in unconditional surrender." But, he added, "unconditional surrender does not mean the extermination or enslavement of the Japanese people." Significantly, and in contrast with his own and Roosevelt's position toward Germany, Truman specified that *only the armed forces* must capitulate unconditionally. The distinction may have been lost on the Japanese, and it may not have been intended by or

10. *FR, Conferences at Malta and Yalta, 1945,* 383–84.
11. *Ibid.,* 384. On September 19, 1944, Roosevelt and Churchill initialed an *aide-mémoire* of a conversation which included the statement, "when a 'bomb' is finally available, it might perhaps, after mature consideration, be used against the Japanese, who should be warned that this bombardment will be repeated until they surrender." *FR, Conference of Berlin (Potsdam), 1945,* II, 1371.

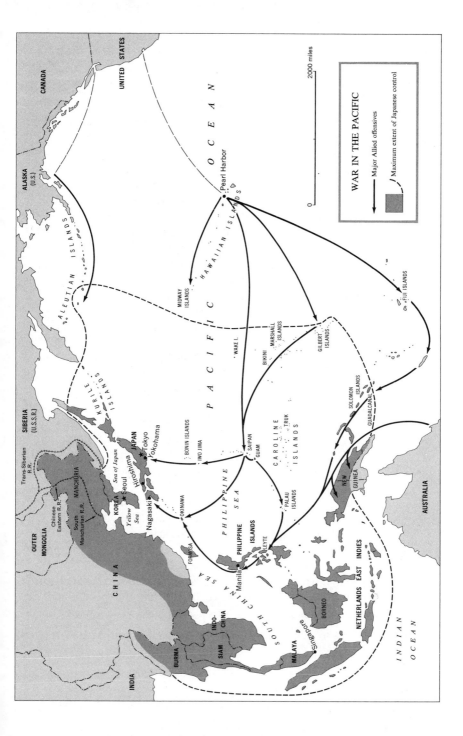

WAR IN THE PACIFIC

Major Allied offensives

Maximum extent of Japanese control

2000 miles

have been apparent to the President, who, on occasion, seemed to employ the term ambiguously. It was not always clear whether he meant political as well as military capitulation. Later in May, Stalin, while approving the announced policy, suggested a modification if it enabled Japan to surrender without a final desperate campaign.[12] A determined effort to induce the President to alter his position was made by Under Secretary of State Joseph C. Grew, long-time ambassador in Tokyo. Stressing the symbolic position of the Emperor and the role of his office in national life, Grew urged that his retention be assured. Although Truman was inclined to make this concession, he felt that circumstances were not propitious for a modification of the doctrine, and he decided to defer a decision until he met with Churchill and Stalin at Potsdam.

The declaration that emerged from this conference notified the Japanese of the fate awaiting them if the war continued and what could be expected if they capitulated. Issued on July 26, 1945, in the names of the Presidents of the United States and the Republic of China and the Prime Minister of Great Britain, the document offered terms from which there were "no alternatives." Officials responsible for aggression were to be removed, Japan was to be occupied and deprived of territories stipulated in the Cairo Declaration, military forces were to be disarmed and mustered out, industry would be permitted as necessary for economic life and the payment of reparations, the Japanese were not to be "enslaved as a race or destroyed as a nation"; but war criminals would be punished and "democratic tendencies" would be encouraged. The final clause called for "the unconditional surrender of all Japanese armed forces," the sole use of this phrase in the proclamation.

The Japanese reaction to this ultimatum as reported to the Western world may not have been what the government, or at least Premier Kantaro Suzuki, intended. The seventy-seven-

12. Harry S. Truman, *Year of Decisions, Memoirs,* Vol. I (Garden City, N.Y., 1955), 265.

year-old Suzuki had taken office in May as a moderate who hopefully could function with the various factions represented in the Cabinet. His colleagues disagreed on the nature of the response and whether any should be made, but Suzuki prevailed on the extremists to *"mokusatsu"* the declaration. Having various connotations in its English translation, the term implied ignoring the proclamation and thereby avoided a confrontation in the Cabinet. It also provided a satisfactory explanation to the public and intimated to the Allies that no decision had been reached on an official reply.[13] The Japanese authorities were still hopeful that earlier requests for Soviet mediation would be fruitful, and Foreign Minister Shigenori Togo optimistically noted that the Potsdam Declaration, unlike those at Casablanca and Cairo, demanded unconditional surrender only of the armed forces.[14]

The President, after waiting what he considered a reasonable length of time for the Japanese government to respond to the Allied offer, and in the absence of any word other than that reported in the press, allowed operations for the utilization of the atomic bombs to proceed. The first was dropped on Hiroshima August 6, 1945, and the second on Nagasaki August 9, 1945. In the midst of these disasters, the Russians, on August 8, informed the Japanese that the two nations were at war. The dilemma facing the Japanese Cabinet was now compounded. On the one hand these new factors made it even more imperative that a way out be found; on the other hand, it seemed even less likely that the Allies would soften the harsh terms of Potsdam. Unable to reach a decision, the Premier and the Cabinet requested an extraordinary Imperial conference which met the evening of August 9.

As each minister presented his position it became apparent that the divergencies of viewpoint were so disparate that no

---

13. For an analysis of the term and its use in this context, see Robert J. C. Butow, *Japan's Decision to Surrender* (Stanford, Calif., 1954), 145–48.

14. *Ibid.*, 144, note 8.

reconciliation was possible. Suzuki, convinced that his country was on the brink of destruction, resorted to the unprecedented step of asking the Emperor to resolve the issue. He, in turn departing from precedent, supported the peace group and rejected the plea from extremists to continue fighting. The next day a dispatch sent to Washington via the Swiss government accepted the terms of the Potsdam Declaration "with the understanding that the said declaration does not comprise any demand which prejudices the prerogatives of His Majesty as a Sovereign Ruler." The American reply stipulated that the Emperor and the Japanese government would be subject to control by the Supreme Commander of the Allied Powers. Again an Imperial conference was called, and again the Emperor decided for peace. When President Truman announced the Japanese response, he declared, "I deem this reply a full acceptance of the Potsdam Declaration which specifies the unconditional surrender of Japan." The great Pacific War was over, the Tokyo government had resorted to unconstitutional action to secure consent to the Allied terms, and the President maintained that the Casablanca formula had not been compromised.[15]

Some writers contend that Japan would have capitulated earlier if it had been made clear that the Emperor could be retained, and claim that the use of nuclear weapons was unnecessary. In fact, Truman has been accused of dropping the bombs not for the purpose of defeating the Japanese but in order to intimidate the Soviet Union by displaying this awesome new American military capability.[16] Yet the unconditional surrender doctrine did not prevent Japan from trying to employ Moscow as an intermediary in the hopes of securing

15. *Public Papers of the Presidents, Harry S Truman, 1945* (Washington, D.C., 1961), 2, 45, 98, 216.
16. Gar Alperovitz, *Atomic Diplomacy: Hiroshima and Potsdam* (New York, 1965). Some of the American leaders were aware of the possible effect this weapon might have on the Kremlin, but there is no substantive evidence to indicate that the President authorized the use of the bomb for this purpose.

a compromise peace. On July 12, 1945, the Japanese ambassador to Moscow was instructed to notify Molotov that Japan wanted to end the war and would send Prince Fumimaro Konoye to Moscow to try to resolve Soviet-Japanese problems. The Russian response was cool, wanting more specific details, and on July 21 the Japanese foreign minister sent another message asking that the Kremlin offer its "good offices" in an effort to terminate the war. On July 28, at Potsdam, Stalin conveyed this information to Truman, who evidently was aware of this exchange because it had been intercepted by the United States.[17] The more specific provisions of the Potsdam document did not mention the future of the Emperor, perhaps deliberately so in light of Truman's earlier inclination to allow his retention.

As to the military justification for the bombs, the Japanese simply were not willing to accept terms that corresponded with the strategic situation. Their outer defense perimeter was in the hands of the enemy, their homeland was under constant bombardment, and the American fleet cruised with impunity in their coastal waters. In spite of this bleak outlook, powerful segments of the government and the armed forces were determined to continue the war, some because they believed the nation was doomed and death was preferable to dishonor, others because a stubborn resistance might produce more favorable peace terms. At this stage the only option left to the Japanese was to prevent an invasion of the home islands, or, if it could not be prevented, to make it so difficult and costly that America would reduce her demands. Nor was this plan so far-fetched. Hoarded for this final battle were an army of two million men and some eight thousand planes of all types. In view of the tenacity with which the Japanese had contested the islands of the southwest Pacific and the frightful destruction wrought on the American Navy at Okinawa by the *kamikaze* suicide planes, the chances for success were not too

17. Butow, *Japan's Decision to Surrender*, 124–27; Truman, *Year of Decisions*, 396–97; *FR, Potsdam Papers*, I, 873; *Ibid.*, II, 1248ff.

dim, and resistance in defense of the mother country was likely to be even more desperate than what had been encountered before.

Furthermore, the authorities in Washington could not know what was happening in the inner circles of the Japanese government. They could assume that an internal struggle was going on, for moderates had moved into the Cabinet, and the overtures to Moscow indicated a desire to terminate the war. But they did not know the extent or nature of the dissension, and they were aware that public exhortations continued to stress victory, that the capacity for significant and determined military resistance remained, and that Japanese fanaticism and the fierce honor code of the armed forces would be at their height in defending the homeland. Following the axiom that one's enemy should be judged by his capabilities rather than his intentions, the American authorities were compelled to expect and plan for the worst. Trying to predict the actions of others is at best a hazardous undertaking, and relying solely on anticipated behavior in war can be disastrous, as the Pearl Harbor attack had revealed. Attempting to probe the legendary inscrutable Oriental mind was even more of a challenge, and the President was subjected to conflicting advice from every side. But no one could present any substantive evidence revealing that the Japanese were on the verge of a surrender that would be acceptable to the Allies. Under the circumstances the President had no viable alternative to authorizing the employment of all the military force at his disposal.

Whether Japan would have capitulated when she did, or soon thereafter, without the impact of the atomic bombs is conjectural. Arguments abound on all sides of the question, but from the record of the Imperial conferences it does seem that this new weapon and the awesome demonstration of its power were an essential factor without which the matter would not have been appealed to the Emperor and without which he would not have taken the position that he did. The shock produced by the bombs was the equivalent of an invasion, and it should be noted that the Emperor in an unprecedented radio address to the people announcing the surrender and explaining the government's action stated: ". . . the enemy has begun to employ a new and most cruel bomb, the power of which to do damage is indeed incalculable, taking the toll of many innocent lives. Should we continue to fight, it would not only result in an ultimate collapse and obliteration of the Japanese nation, but also it would lead to the total extinction of civilization." [18] Also, the nuclear weapons probably enabled some of the Japanese military hierarchy to accept defeat without losing face, for this was a technological device which they did not possess and with which they could not be expected to compete.

But a judgment of the President's decision requires a consideration of other factors that he could not ignore. The assertion that his primary motive was to intimidate Russia would be credible only if his other responsibilities were neglected, including the circumstances in which he operated. That he was influenced, at least, by the atmosphere which prevailed when he took office is undeniable. Truman had inherited an elaborate and expensive program, and its momentum was virtually irreversible. Could he deny its fulfillment to the taxpayers and the Congress and write it off as a noble experiment warranted by the prospect that the other side might produce its equivalent? [19] Again, there is no evidence to indicate that the President felt any compulsion to validate a highly speculative government project by such a vivid demonstration of its results. That he may have been caught up in the intricate preparations for the utilization of this weapon is more credible, although he received information and counsel on the

18. Butow, *Japan's Decision to Surrender,* 3.
19. This point is stressed by Len Giovannitti and Fred Freed, *The Decision to Drop the Bomb* (New York, 1965), namely, "At the most pragmatic level, if it were not used Congress and the public would ask angry questions about the expenditure of two billion dollars for a weapon that was then withheld from combat." *Ibid.,* 316.

various ramifications of the bomb from his advisers and from a special committee headed by Secretary of War Henry Stimson. Composed of government officials and distinguished scientists, this group recommended that the weapon be used against the enemy without delay. At the top level there seemed to be no compunctions about using the bomb. It was regarded as a legitimate military device to be employed against the foe, another form of violence in the arsenal of modern weaponry. While other motives may have been present in the minds of some of the authorities, the advice and the decision were based on the exigencies of the military situation.[20]

In retrospect the atomic bomb helped achieve immediate military and political objectives. It must have made an impression on the Russians, who were aware that the United States possessed this most destructive weapon and actually had used it. If, as contended here, the bomb shortened the war and helped prevent an invasion of Japan, it was responsible for saving many lives on all sides and depriving Russia of a share in occupying that country, an occupation which may have produced a divided nation similar to Germany and Korea. The moral or ethical side of the issue is more troublesome, particularly in light of the fire raids on Tokyo and the bombings of Hamburg and Dresden, which killed, in each case, more people than died in either of the atomic attacks. An industrial society provides more efficient methods for bringing death and destruction to the enemy, which is the criterion for success in warfare.[21]

Among the more unfortunate results of Hiroshima and Nagasaki was the psychological impact. The United States

20. In addition to the aforementioned books, see Herbert Feis, *The Atomic Bomb and the End of World War II* (Princeton, 1966), a revision of his earlier work, *Japan Subdued: The Atomic Bomb and the End of the War in the Pacific* (Princeton, 1961).

21. For nonmilitary implications of the nuclear attack, see Robert Jay Lifton, "Psychological Effects of the Atomic Bomb in Hiroshima: The Theme of Death," *Daedalus,* 92 (Summer 1963), 462–97.

was the first, and so far has been the only, nation to employ these weapons, and they were used against an Oriental people. The repercussions of this experience have been widespread and will probably endure for generations. America did not enter the nuclear age with clean hands.

6

Conclusion

THE DEATH and destruction wrought by World War II is impressive even in an age inured to the speculative effects of a thermonuclear holocaust. Approximately seventeen million killed in battle, over eighteen million civilian deaths resulting directly or indirectly from the carnage. The military costs amounted to a trillion dollars, and material destruction came to at least twice that figure. An expensive operation for both victor and vanquished. These casualties and the truly global dimensions of the war give some indication of the magnitude and complexity of this massive struggle. What is often lost in retrospect is an appreciation of the human effort that went into the administering, planning, and waging of the war. Too often mistakes are emphasized, and it has been remarked that in reading much of the literature it appears that nothing anyone did was right. Nor is it necessary to believe that war is the supreme test of a nation's—or a person's—spirit, or that war is man's noblest form of activity. This conflict made demands that could be met only by an exercise of skill and determination seldom exacted or revealed in other activities. It demonstrated that humankind was capable of resolving a great many of its problems if a similar dedication and cooperation were applied in more peaceful pursuits.

Also forgotten in retrospect is the simple truth that the Allies could have lost the war. Errors in judgment, faulty strategy, and chance or luck were among the factors that influenced battles, campaigns, and the final outcome. But one single factor which virtually would have assured Axis success or at least a compromise peace would have been a split among the Allies. The alliance was at best tenuous, with mutual suspicions and conflicting aspirations. Differences over military operations and postwar settlements at times threatened to disrupt the coalition, and each of the leaders, realizing that unity was imperative for victory, made concessions when it appeared that a break was possible. Harmony was maintained in spite of some fundamental disagreement over military strategy. It is doubtful that the association would have continued if there had been an early dispute over basic war aims. Perhaps this was the greatest value of the unconditional surrender policy, for it deferred a formal confrontation on specifics until Germany's defeat was assured. The formula was, as one writer puts it, "a lowest common denominator to which the Allies could subscribe." [1]

That the formula made other contributions to the winning of the war is undeniable. On the home front it prevented a good deal of the bickering over surrender terms that had plagued Wilson; and Senator Burton K. Wheeler, the former New Deal enthusiast, was one of the few critics of the doctrine in Congress, and probably the most outspoken. It helped mollify domestic indignation over the "deal" consummated with Admiral Darlan in the North African operation, when it seemed to many liberals that Roosevelt was willing to compromise with Fascist-type leaders. The "slogan" enabled Roosevelt to devote the greater part of his energies to the first priority, winning the war, while it minimized the amount of attention he had to devote to public assurances on war aims. The delay also enabled his advisers to prepare the elaborate studies and provide the consultation for the incredibly numer-

---

1. John P. Glennon, " 'This Time Germany Is a Defeated Nation': The Doctrine of Unconditional Surrender and Some Unsuccessful Attempts to Alter It, 1943–1944," in Gerald N. Grob, ed., *Statesmen and Statecraft of the Modern West: Essays in Honor of Dwight E. Lee and H. Donaldson Jordan* (Barre, Mass., 1967), 143.

ous and complex decisions that peace would demand. The President understandably changed his mind on numerous issues, and he did not want to be committed at an early stage to policies which information, circumstances, or other factors might prove undesirable or impracticable.

Maintaining flexibility in political affairs was an intrinsic purpose of the unconditional surrender policy, both to preserve the alliance during the war and to ensure its continuance in the forthcoming peace. Especially applicable to Germany and Japan to prevent a quarrel among the Allies over terms or subsequent recriminations or excuses by the defeated foe, it gave the victors a free hand in creating the kind of world they wanted without having to consult their erstwhile enemies. Differences over postwar settlements within the coalition were such that the added complication of negotiating with the Germans and Japanese might have made agreement impossible. Bargaining with the vanquished would have opened the way for an exploitation of the conflicting ambitions of the victors with dire implications for the future. The President, contrary to many allegations, was primarily concerned with the conditions of the peace. He was determined to reduce as much as possible the circumstances in which the roots of war could flourish, and he endorsed the Wilsonian concept of collective security as the best hope to deter and resist aggression. No nation, he believed, was immune from the contagion of war, and control was possible only through the concerted action of the major powers. Each had its role to play and each was an essential ingredient in the maintenance of peace. The unconditional surrender formula provided an operational objective within which the indispensable and desirable aims of the Allies could be negotiated. Although the line separating these two categories was often indistinct, each of the Big Three managed to avoid an implacable adherence to any position that alienated one or both of the others.

Experienced politicians, leaders of their nations during the most critical and demanding times, these men were not inclined to write off the sacrifices of their people and relinquish what they considered the legitimate fruits of victory. Concessions to their comrades-in-arms were made within the framework of perceived national interests, the military situation, publicly declared general objectives, and the extent of the contribution to the war effort. Since these considerations were often contradictory and not all were reducible to quantifiable data, the task confronting these chosen few was of such magnitude that it defies the imagination. The compromises made by the Soviet Union, and there were many, were confined to issues that did not directly affect the safety and security of the nation. Those made by the Western Allies were based primarily on the realization that they were in no position to do otherwise. The military situation on the Continent certainly influenced, if it did not determine, much of the policy that was to prevail in Central and Eastern Europe following the war.

In assessing the political consequences of the war it could be argued that the accomplishments of each of the three Allied nations were commensurate with their military contribution to the defeat of the principal enemy, Germany. In this respect, and in regard to the diplomacy of the war, this narrative has been critical of Churchill. It was the Prime Minister who pressed for early and generous agreements with the Russians, who urged that the victorious powers be given their choice of the spoils, who insisted on dividing southeastern Europe into spheres of influence, who established occupation zones, who belatedly perceived a Soviet menace in Europe, and who was responsible for the indirect strategy which delayed a cross-channel invasion and placed the Western Allies in a weaker bargaining position when postwar arrangements were being negotiated. The peripheral approach was neither militarily nor politically sound. Militarily, this strategy lengthened the war, demanded the commitment of more resources, and increased casualties on all sides. Politically, it created dissension among the Allies, provoked distrust, and strengthened Russia's hand. Perhaps the most telling criticism that can be leveled against

Roosevelt is that too often he yielded to the Prime Minister in these matters.

It seems obvious that in many respects Britain was a more difficult ally than Russia, and without the warm personal relationship that developed between the President and Churchill one of the many opportunities for a basic altercation could have materialized. Roosevelt, in his dealings with the mercurial Churchill and the taciturn Stalin, may have shifted with the prevailing winds, but he maintained a steady course. One need not agree with A. J. P. Taylor's verdict that "Of the three great men at the top, Roosevelt was the only one who knew what he was doing." [2] But he did adhere to his two major goals: the elimination of the Axis peril and the creation of a framework for a new international order. Both of these objectives were realized, and the unconditional surrender doctrine was instrumental in the achievement of this grand design.

2. A. J. P. Taylor, *English History, 1914–1945* (New York, 1965), 577.

Appendices

A Bibliographic Review

Index

Appendices

Appendix A: Atlantic Charter

Joint Statement by President Roosevelt and Prime Minister Churchill. August 14, 1941. (*Foreign Relations, 1941,* I, 367–69)

The following statement signed by the President of the United States and the Prime Minister of Great Britain is released for the information of the Press:

The President of the United States and the Prime Minister, Mr. Churchill, representing His Majesty's Government in the United Kingdom, have met at sea.

They have been accompanied by officials of their two Governments, including high ranking officers of their Military, Naval and Air Services.

The whole problem of the supply of munitions of war, as provided by the Lease-Lend Act, for the armed forces of the United States and for those countries actively engaged in resisting aggression has been further examined.

Lord Beaverbrook, the Minister of Supply of the British Government, has joined in these conferences. He is going to proceed to Washington to discuss further details with appropriate officials of the United States Government. These conferences will also cover the supply problems of the Soviet Union.

The President and the Prime Minister have had several conferences. They have considered the dangers to world civilization arising from the policies of military domination by conquest upon

which the Hitlerite government of Germany and other governments associated therewith have embarked, and have made clear
the steps which their countries are respectively taking for their
safety in the face of these dangers.

They have agreed upon the following joint declaration:

Joint declaration of the President of the United States of
America and the Prime Minister, Mr. Churchill, representing His
Majesty's Government in the United Kingdom, being met together,
deem it right to make known certain common principles in the
national policies of their respective countries on which they base
their hopes for a better future for the world.

First, their countries seek no aggrandizement, territorial or
other;

Second, they desire to see no territorial changes that do not
accord with the freely expressed wishes of the peoples concerned;

Third, they respect the right of all peoples to choose the form
of government under which they will live; and they wish to see
sovereign rights and self government restored to those who have
been forcibly deprived of them;

Fourth, they will endeavor, with due respect for their existing
obligations, to further the enjoyment by all States, great or small,
victor or vanquished, of access, on equal terms, to the trade and
to the raw materials of the world which are needed for their economic prosperity;

Fifth, they desire to bring about the fullest collaboration between all nations in the economic field with the object of securing
for all, improved labor standards, economic advancement and
social security;

Sixth, after the final destruction of the Nazi tyranny, they
hope to see established a peace which will afford to all nations the
means of dwelling in safety within their own boundaries, and which
will afford assurance that all the men in all the lands may live out
their lives in freedom from fear and want;

Seventh, such a peace should enable all men to traverse the
high seas and oceans without hindrance;

Eighth, they believe that all of the nations of the world, for
realistic as well as spiritual reasons must come to the abandonment of the use of force. Since no future peace can be maintained
if land, sea or air armaments continue to be employed by nations

which threaten, or may threaten, aggression outside of their frontiers, they believe, pending the establishment of a wider and permanent system of general security, that the disarmament of such nations is essential. They will likewise aid and encourage all other practicable measures which will lighten for peace-loving peoples the crushing burden of armaments.

Franklin D. Roosevelt
Winston S. Churchill

Appendix B: United Nations Declaration

A Joint Declaration by the United States of America, the United Kingdom of Great Britain and Northern Ireland, the Union of Soviet Socialist Republics, China, Australia, Belgium, Canada, Costa Rica, Cuba, Czechoslovakia, Dominican Republic, El Salvador, Greece, Guatemala, Haiti, Honduras, India, Luxembourg, Netherlands, New Zealand, Nicaragua, Norway, Panama, Poland, South Africa, Yugoslavia. Washington. January 1, 1942. (*Foreign Relations, 1942*, I, 25–26)

The Governments signatory hereto,

Having subscribed to a common program of purposes and principles embodied in the Joint Declaration of the President of the United States of America and the Prime Minister of the United Kingdom of Great Britain and Northern Ireland dated August 14, 1941, known as the Atlantic Charter.

Being convinced that complete victory over their enemies is essential to defend life, liberty, independence and religious freedom, and to preserve human rights and justice in their own lands as well as in other lands, and that they are now engaged in a common struggle against savage and brutal forces seeking to subjugate the world,

DECLARE:

(1) Each Government pledges itself to employ its full resources, military or economic, against those members of the Tri-

partite Pact and its adherents with which such government is at war.

(2) Each Government pledges itself to cooperate with the Governments signatory hereto and not to make a separate armistice or peace with the enemies.

The foregoing declaration may be adhered to by other nations which are, or which may be, rendering material assistance and contributions in the struggle for victory over Hitlerism.

Done at Washington
January First, 1942.

Appendix C: Surrender of Italy

Instrument of Armistice and surrender of the Italian Forces to the Commander-in-Chief of the Allied Forces, General Dwight D. Eisenhower. Sicily. September 3, 1943. (U.S. Senate, *Surrender of Italy, Germany and Japan* [Doc. 93, 79th Cong. 1st ses.], Washington, D.C., 1946)

The following conditions of an Armistice are presented by General Dwight D. Eisenhower, Commander-in-Chief of the Allied Forces, acting by authority of the Governments of the United States and Great Britain and in the interest of the United Nations, and are accepted by Marshal Pietro Badoglio, Head of the Italian Government:

1. Immediate cessation of all hostile activity by the Italian armed forces.

2. Italy will use its best endeavors to deny, to the Germans, facilities that might be used against the United Nations.

3. All prisoners or internees of the United Nations to be immediately turned over to the Allied Commander-in-Chief, and none of these may now or at any time be evacuated to Germany.

4. Immediate transfer of the Italian Fleet and Italian aircraft to such points as may be designated by the Allied Commander-in-Chief, with details of disarmament to be prescribed by him.

5. Italian merchant shipping may be requisitioned by the Allied Commander-in-Chief to meet the needs of his military-naval program.

6. Immediate surrender of Corsica and of all Italian territory, both islands and mainland, to the Allies, for such use as operational bases and other purposes as the Allies may see fit.

7. Immediate guarantee of the free use by the Allies of all airfields and naval ports in Italian territory, regardless of the rate of evacuation of the Italian territory by the German forces. These ports and fields to be protected by Italian armed forces until this function is taken over by the Allies.

8. Immediate withdrawal to Italy of Italian armed forces from all participation in the current war from whatever areas in which they may now be engaged.

9. Guarantee by the Italian Government that if necessary it will employ all its available armed forces to insure prompt and exact compliance with all the provisions of this armistice.

10. The Commander-in-Chief of the Allied Forces reserves to himself the right to take any measure which in his opinion may be necessary for the protection of the interests of the Allied Forces for the prosecution of the war, and the Italian Government binds itself to take such administrative or other action as the Commander-in-Chief may require, and in particular the Commander-in-Chief will establish Allied Military Government over such parts of Italian territory as he may deem necessary in the military interests of the Allied Nations.

11. The Commander-in-Chief of the Allied Forces will have a full right to impose measures of disarmament, demobilization and demilitarization.

12. Other conditions of a political, economic and financial nature with which Italy will be bound to comply will be transmitted at later date.

The conditions of the present Armistice will not be made public without prior approval of the Allied Commander-in-Chief. The English will be considered the official text.

Marshal Pietro Badoglio
Head of the Italian Government

By: Giuseppe Castellano

Brigadier General, attached to
The Italian High Command

Dwight D. Eisenhower
General, U. S. Army
Commander in Chief Allied Forces

By: Walter B. Smith
Major General, U. S. Army
Chief of Staff

Proclamation by General Eisenhower on the Italian Surrender.
United Nations Radio, September 8, 1943.

This is Gen. Dwight D. Eisenhower, Commander in Chief of the Allied Forces.

The Italian Government has surrendered its armed forces unconditionally. As Allied Commander in Chief, I have granted a military armistice, the terms of which have been approved by the Governments of the United Kingdom, the United States and the Union of Soviet Socialist Republics. Thus I am acting in the interest of the United Nations.

The Italian Government has bound itself to abide by these terms without reservation. The armistice was signed by my representative and the representative of Marshal Badoglio and it becomes effective this instant.

Hostilities between the armed forces of the United Nations and those of Italy terminate at once. All Italians who now act to help eject the German aggressor from Italian soil will have the assistance and the support of the United Nations.

Appendix D: Surrender of Germany

Declaration of Four Nations on General Security, following the Moscow Conference of Foreign Ministers, October 18–November 1, 1943. (*Foreign Relations, 1943,* I, 755–56)

The Governments of the United States of America, the United Kingdom, the Soviet Union and China;

united in their determination, in accordance with the Declaration by the United Nations of January 1, 1942, and subsequent declarations, to continue hostilities against those Axis powers with which they respectively are at war until such powers have laid down their arms on the basis of unconditional surrender;

conscious of their responsibility to secure the liberation of themselves and the peoples allied with them from the menace of aggression;

recognizing the necessity of ensuring a rapid and orderly transition from war to peace and of establishing and maintaining international peace and security with the least diversion of the world's human and economic resources for armaments;

jointly declare:

1. That their united action, pledged for the prosecution of the war against their respective enemies, will be continued for the organization and maintenance of peace and security.

2. That those of them at war with a common enemy will act together in all matters relating to the surrender and disarmament of that enemy.

3. That they will take all measures deemed by them to be necessary to provide against any violation of the terms imposed upon the enemy.

4. That they recognize the necessity of establishing at the earliest practicable date a general international organization, based on the principle of the sovereign equality of all peace-loving states, and open to membership by all such states, large and small, for

the maintenance of international peace and security.

5. That for the purposes of maintaining international peace and security pending the reestablishment of law and order and the inauguration of a system of general security, they will consult with one another and as occasion requires with other members of the United Nations with a view to joint action on behalf of the community of nations.

6. That after the termination of hostilities they will not employ their military forces within the territories of other states except for the purposes envisaged in this declaration and after joint consultation.

7. That they will confer and cooperate with one another and with other members of the United Nations to bring about a practicable general agreement with respect to the regulation of armaments in the post-war period.

Instrument of Surrender of all German Forces to General Dwight D. Eisenhower, Supreme Commander of the Allied Expeditionary Forces, and to the Soviet High Command. Rheims. May 7, 1945. (U.S. Senate, *Surrender of Italy, Germany and Japan*)

1. We the undersigned, acting by authority of the German High Command, hereby surrender unconditionally to the Supreme Commander, Allied Expeditionary Force and simultaneously to the Soviet High Command all forces on land, sea, and in the air who are at this date under German control.

2. The German High Command will at once issue orders to all German military, naval and air authorities and to all forces under German control to cease active operations at 2301 hours Central European time on 8 May and to remain in the positions occupied at that time. No ship, vessel, or aircraft is to be scuttled, or any damage done to their hull, machinery or equipment.

3. The German High Command will at once issue to the appropriate commanders, and ensure the carrying out of any further orders issued by the Supreme Commander, Allied Expedi-

ionary Force and by the Soviet High Command.

4. This act of military surrender is without prejudice to, and will be superseded by any general instrument of surrender imposed by, or on behalf of the United Nations and applicable to GERMANY and the German armed forces as a whole.

5. In the event of the German High Command or any of the forces under their control failing to act in accordance with this Act of Surrender, the Supreme Commander, Allied Expeditionary Force and the Soviet High Command will take such punitive or other action as they deem appropriate.

Signed at Rheims at 0241 on the 7th day of May, 1945.

France
On behalf of the German High Command.
    Jodl

IN THE PRESENCE OF:

On behalf of the Supreme Commander,
Allied Expeditionary Force
W. B. Smith
F. Sevez

Major General, French Army
    (Witness)

On behalf of the Soviet High Command
Sousloparov

Instrument of Surrender of all German Forces to the Supreme Commander of the Allied Expeditionary Force, General Dwight D. Eisenhower, and to the Supreme High Command of the Red Army. Berlin. May 8, 1945.

1. We the undersigned, acting by authority of the German High Command, hereby surrender unconditionally to the Supreme Commander, Allied Expeditionary Force and simultaneously to the Supreme High Command of the Red Army all forces on land, at sea, and in the air who are at this date under German control.

2. The German High Command will at once issue orders to all German military, naval and air authorities and to all forces under German control to cease active operations at 2301 hours Central European time on 8th May 1945, to remain in the positions occupied at that time and to disarm completely, handing over their weapons and equipment to the local allied commanders or officers designated by Representatives of the Allied Supreme Commands. No ship, vessel, or aircraft is to be scuttled, or any damage done to their hull, machinery or equipment, and also to machines of all kinds, armament, apparatus, and all the technical means of prosecution of war in general.

3. The German High Command will at once issue to the appropriate commanders, and ensure the carrying out of any further orders issued by the Supreme Commander, Allied Expeditionary Force and by the Supreme High Command of the Red Army.

4. This act of military surrender is without prejudice to, and will be superseded by any general instrument of surrender imposed by, or on behalf of the United Nations and applicable to GERMANY and the German armed forces as a whole.

5. In the event of the German High Command or any of the forces under their control failing to act in accordance with this Act of Surrender, the Supreme Commander, Allied Expeditionary Force and the Supreme High Command of the Red Army will take such punitive or other action as they deem appropriate.

6. This Act is drawn up in the English, Russian and German languages. The English and Russian are the only authentic texts.

Signed at Berlin on the 8. day of May, 1945

Friedeburg   Keitel   Stumpf
On behalf of the German High Command

IN THE PRESENCE OF:

On behalf of the Supreme Commander
Allied Expeditionary Force
A. W. Tedder

At the signing also were present as witnesses:

F. de Lattre-Tassigny
General Commanding in Chief First French Army

On behalf of the Supreme High Command of the Red Army
G. Zhukov
Carl Spaatz
General, Commanding United States Strategic Air Forces

Proclamation by General Eisenhower on the unconditional surrender of Germany. Paris. May 8, 1945.

In 1943 the late President Roosevelt and Premier [*sic*] Churchill met in Casablanca. There they pronounced the formula of unconditional surrender for the Axis Powers.

In Europe that formula has now been fulfilled. The Allied force which invaded Europe on June 6, 1944, has, with its great Russian ally and the forces advancing from the south, utterly defeated the Germans on land, sea and air.

This unconditional surrender has been achieved by team-work, team-work not only among all the Allies participating but among all the services, land, sea and air.

To every subordinate that has been in this command of almost 5,000,000 Allies I owe a debt of gratitude that can never be repaid. The only repayment that can be made to them is the deep appreciation and lasting gratitude of all the free citizens of all the United Nations.

Statement by President Truman on the surrender of Nazi Germany. The White House. May 8, 1945.

Nazi Germany has been defeated.

The Japanese people have felt the weight of our land, air, and naval attacks. So long as their leaders and the armed forces continue the war the striking power and intensity of our blows will steadily increase and will bring utter destruction to Japan's industrial war production, to its shipping, and to everything that supports its military activity.

The longer the war lasts, the greater will be the suffering and hardships which the people of Japan will undergo—all in vain. Our blows will not cease until the Japanese military and naval forces lay down their arms in *unconditional surrender.*

Just what does the unconditional surrender of the armed forces mean for the Japanese people?

It means the end of the war.

It means the termination of the influence of the military leaders who have brought Japan to the present brink of disaster.

It means provision for the return of soldiers and sailors to their families, their farms, their jobs.

It means not prolonging the present agony and suffering of the Japanese in the vain hope of victory.

Unconditional surrender does not mean the extermination or enslavement of the Japanese people.

Appendix E: Surrender of Japan

Statement issued by President Roosevelt, Generalissimo Chiang-Kai-shek, and Prime Minister Winston Churchill, following the Cairo Conference of November 22–26, 1943. (*Department of State Bulletin,* IX, 393)

The several military missions have agreed upon future military operations against Japan. The Three Great Allies expressed their resolve to bring unrelenting pressure against their brutal enemies by sea, land, and air. This pressure is already rising.

The Three Great Allies are fighting this war to restrain and punish the aggression of Japan. They covet no gain for themselves and have no thought of territorial expansion. It is their purpose that Japan shall be stripped of all the islands in the Pacific which she has seized or occupied since the beginning of the first World War in 1914, and that all the territories Japan has stolen from the Chinese, such as Manchuria, Formosa, and the Pescadores, shall be restored to the Republic of China. Japan will also be expelled from all other territories which she has taken by violence and greed. The aforesaid three great powers, mindful of the enslavement of the people of Korea, are determined that in due course Korea shall become free and independent.

With these objects in view the three Allies, in harmony with those of the United Nations at war with Japan, will continue to persevere in the serious and prolonged operations necessary to procure the unconditional surrender of Japan.

Agreement regarding the Far East from the document signed by President Roosevelt, Marshal Stalin, and Prime Minister Churchill. Yalta. February 11, 1945. (*Foreign Relations: The Conferences at Malta and Yalta, 1945,* 984)

The leaders of the three Great Powers—the Soviet Union, the United States of America and Great Britain—have agreed that in two or three months after Germany has surrendered and the war in Europe has terminated the Soviet Union shall enter into the war against Japan on the side of the Allies on condition that:

1. The status quo in Outer-Mongolia (The Mongolian People's Republic) shall be preserved;

2. The former rights of Russia violated by the treacherous attack of Japan in 1904 shall be restored, viz:

(a) the southern part of Sakhalin as well as all the islands adjacent to it shall be returned to the Soviet Union,

(b) the commercial port of Dairen shall be internationalized, the preeminent interests of the Soviet Union in this port being safeguarded and the lease of Port Arthur as a naval base of the U.S.S.R. restored,

(c) The Chinese-Eastern Railroad and the South-Manchurian Railroad which provides an outlet to Dairen shall be jointly operated by the establishment of a joint Soviet-Chinese Company it being understood that the preeminent interests of the Soviet Union shall be safeguarded and that China shall retain full sovereignty in Manchuria;

3. The Kuril islands shall be handed over to the Soviet Union. It is understood, that the agreement concerning Outer-Mon-

golia and the ports and the railroads referred to above will require concurrence of Generalissimo Chiang Kai-shek. The President will take measures in order to obtain this concurrence on advice from Marshal Stalin.

The Heads of the three Great Powers have agreed that these claims of the Soviet Union shall be unquestionably fulfilled after Japan has been defeated.

For its part the Soviet Union expresses its readiness to conclude with the National Government of China a pact of friendship and alliance between the U.S.S.R. and China in order to render assistance to China with its armed forces for the purpose of liberating China from the Japanese yoke.

Potsdam Declaration, signed by President Truman, Prime Minister Churchill, and concurred in by Chiang Kai-shek, President of the National Government of China, calling on the Japanese to surrender unconditionally. Potsdam. July 26, 1945. (U.S. Senate, *Surrender of Italy, Germany and Japan*)

(1) We—the President of the United States, the President of the National Government of the Republic of China, and the Prime Minister of Great Britain, representing the hundreds of millions of our countrymen, have conferred and agree that Japan shall be given an opportunity to end this war.

(2) The prodigious land, sea and air forces of the United States, the British Empire and of China, many times reinforced by their armies and air fleets from the west, are poised to strike the final blows upon Japan. This military power is sustained and inspired by the determination of all the Allied Nations to prosecute the war against Japan until she ceases to resist.

(3) The result of the futile and senseless German resistance to the might of the aroused free peoples of the world stands forth in awful clarity as an example to the people of Japan. The might that now converges on Japan is immeasurably greater than that which, when applied to the resisting Nazis, necessarily laid waste to the lands, the industry and the method of life of the whole

German people. The full application of our military power, backed by our resolve, *will* mean the inevitable and complete destruction of the Japanese armed forces and just as inevitably the utter devastation of the Japanese homeland.

(4) The time has come for Japan to decide whether she will continue to be controlled by those self-willed militaristic advisers whose unintelligent calculations have brought the Empire of Japan to the threshold of annihilation, or whether she will follow the path of reason.

(5) Following are our terms. We will not deviate from them. There are no alternatives. We shall brook no delay.

(6) There must be eliminated for all time the authority and influence of those who have deceived and misled the people of Japan into embarking on world conquest, for we insist that a new order of peace, security and justice will be impossible until irresponsible militarism is driven from the world.

(7) Until such a new order is established *and* until there is convincing proof that Japan's war-making power is destroyed, points in Japanese territory to be designated by the Allies shall be occupied to secure the achievement of the basic objectives we are here setting forth.

(8) The terms of the Cairo Declaration shall be carried out and Japanese sovereignty shall be limited to the islands of Honshu, Hokkaido, Kyushu, Shikoku and such minor islands as we determine.

(9) The Japanese military forces, after being completely disarmed, shall be permitted to return to their homes with the opportunity to lead peaceful and productive lives.

(10) We do not intend that the Japanese shall be enslaved as a race or destroyed as a nation, but stern justice shall be meted out to all war criminals, including those who have visited cruelties upon our prisoners. The Japanese Government shall remove all obstacles to the revival and strengthening of democratic tendencies among the Japanese people. Freedom of speech, of religion, and of thought, as well as respect for the fundamental human rights shall be established.

(11) Japan shall be permitted to maintain such industries as will sustain her economy and permit the exaction of just reparations in kind, but not those which would enable her to re-arm for war.

To this end, access to, as distinguished from control of, raw materials shall be permitted. Eventual Japanese participation in world trade relations shall be permitted.

(12) The occupying forces of the Allies shall be withdrawn from Japan as soon as these objectives have been accomplished and there has been established in accordance with the freely expressed will of the Japanese people a peacefully inclined and responsible government.

(13) We call upon the government of Japan to proclaim now the unconditional surrender of all Japanese armed forces, and to provide proper and adequate assurances of their good faith in such action. The alternative for Japan is prompt and utter destruction.

Japanese offer of surrender, exchange of correspondence between the Secretary of State, James F. Byrnes, and Max Grässli, Chargé d'Affaires ad interim of Switzerland. August 10–14, 1945.

Grässli letter of August 10, 1945

Sir:

I have the honor to inform you that the Japanese Minister to Switzerland, upon instructions received from his Government, has requested the Swiss Political Department to advise the Government of the United States of America of the following:

"In obedience to the gracious command of His Majesty the Emperor who, ever anxious to enhance the cause of world peace, desires earnestly to bring about a speedy termination of hostilities with a view to saving mankind from the calamities to be imposed upon them by further continuation of the war, the Japanese Government several weeks ago asked the Soviet Government, with which neutral relations then prevailed, to render good offices in restoring peace vis à vis the enemy powers. Unfortunately, these efforts in the interest of peace having failed, the Japanse Government in conformity with the august wish of His Majesty to restore the general peace and desiring to put an end to the untold sufferings entailed by war as quickly as possible, have decided upon the following:

"The Japanese Government are ready to accept the terms enumerated in the joint declaration which was issued at Potsdam on July 26th, 1945, by the heads of the Governments of the United States, Great Britain, and China, and later subscribed by the Soviet Government, with the understanding that the said declaration does not comprise any demand which prejudices the prerogatives of His Majesty as a Sovereign Ruler.

"The Japanese Government sincerely hope that this understanding is warranted and desire keenly that an explicit indication to that effect will be speedily forthcoming."

In transmitting the above message the Japanese Minister added that his Government begs the Government of the United States to forward its answer through the intermediary of Switzerland. Similar requests are being transmitted to the Governments of Great Britain and the Union of Soviet Socialist Republics through the intermediary of Sweden, as well as to the Government of China through the intermediary of Switzerland. The Chinese Minister at Berne has already been informed of the foregoing through the channel of the Swiss Political Department.

Please be assured that I am at your disposal at any time to accept for and forward to my Government the reply of the Government of the United States.

Accept [etc.]

> Grässli
> *Chargé d'Affaires ad interim*
> *of Switzerland*

Byrnes reply of August 11, 1945

Sir:

I have the honor to acknowledge receipt of your note of August 10, and in reply to inform you that the President of the United States has directed me to send to you for transmission by your Government to the Japanese Government the following message on behalf of the Governments of the United States, the United Kingdom, the Union of Soviet Socialist Republics, and China:

"With regard to the Japanese Government's message accepting the terms of the Potsdam proclamation, but containing the statement, 'with the understanding that the said declaration does not comprise any demand which prejudices the prerogatives of His Majesty as a sovereign ruler,' our position is as follows:

"From the moment of surrender the authority of the Emperor and the Japanese Government to rule the state shall be subject to the Supreme Commander of the Allied powers who will take such steps as he deems proper to effectuate the surrender terms.

"The Emperor will be required to authorize and ensure the signature by the Government of Japan and the Japanese Imperial General Headquarters of the surrender terms necessary to carry out the provisions of the Potsdam Declaration, and shall issue his commands to all the Japanese military, naval and air authorities and to all the forces under their control wherever located to cease active operations and to surrender their arms, and to issue such other orders as the Supreme Commander may require to give effect to the surrender terms.

"Immediately upon the surrender the Japanese Government shall transport prisoners of war and civilian internees to places of safety, as directed, where they can quickly be placed aboard Allied transports.

"The ultimate form of government of Japan shall, in accordance with the Potsdam Declaration, be established by the freely expressed will of the Japanese people.

"The armed forces of the Allied Powers will remain in Japan until the purposes set forth in the Potsdam Declaration are achieved."

Accept [etc.]

James F. Byrnes
Secretary of State

Grässli letter of August 14, 1945
Sir:

I have the honor to refer to your note of August 11, in which you requested me to transmit to my Government the reply of the Governments of the United States, the United Kingdom, the Union of Soviet Socialist Republics, and China to the message from the Japanese Government which was communicated in my note of August 10.

At 20.10 today (Swiss Time) the Japanese Minister to Switzerland conveyed the following written statement to the Swiss Government for transmission to the four Allied governments:

"Communication of the Japanese Government of August 14, 1945, addressed to the Governments of the United States, Great Britain, the Soviet Union, and China:

"With reference to the Japanese Government's note of August 10 regarding their acceptance of the provisions of the Potsdam declaration and the reply of the Governments of the United States, Great Britain, the Soviet Union, and China sent by American Secretary of State Byrnes under the date of August 11, the Japanese Government have the honor to communicate to the Governments of the four powers as follows:

"1. His Majesty the Emperor has issued an Imperial rescript regarding Japan's acceptance of the provisions of the Potsdam declaration.

"2. His Majesty the Emperor is prepared to authorize and ensure the signature by his Government and the Imperial General Headquarters of the necessary terms for carrying out the provisions of the Potsdam declaration. His Majesty is also prepared to issue his commands to all the military, naval, and air authorities of Japan and all the forces under their control wherever located to cease active operations, to surrender arms and to issue such other orders as may be required by the Supreme Commander of the Allied Forces for the execution of the above-mentioned terms."

Accept [etc.]

Grässli
Chargé d'Affaires ad interim
of Switzerland

Byrnes reply of August 14, 1945

Sir:

With reference to your communication of today's date, transmitting the reply of the Japanese Government to the communication which I sent through you to the Japanese Government on

August 11, on behalf of the Governments of the United States, China, the United Kingdom, and the Union of Soviet Socialist Republics, which I regard as full acceptance of the Potsdam Declaration and of my statement of August 11, 1945, I have the honor to inform you that the President of the United States has directed that the following message be sent to you for transmission to the Japanese Government:

"You are to proceed as follows:

"(1) Direct prompt cessation of hostilities by Japanese forces, informing the Supreme Commander for the Allied Powers of the effective date and hour of such cessation.

"(2) Send emissaries at once to the Supreme Commander for the Allied Powers with information of the disposition of the Japanese forces and commanders, and fully empowered to make any arrangements directed by the Supreme Commander for the Allied Powers to enable him and his accompanying forces to arrive at the place designated by him to receive the formal surrender.

"(3) For the purpose of receiving such surrender and carrying it into effect, General of the Army Douglas MacArthur has been designated as the Supreme Commander for the Allied Powers, and he will notify the Japanese Government of the time, place and other details of the formal surrender."

Accept [etc.]

James F. Byrnes
Secretary of State

Statement by President Truman on the Japanese notes accepting the terms of the Potsdam Declaration. Washington. August 14, 1945. (U.S. Senate, *Surrender of Italy, Germany and Japan*)

I have received this afternoon a message from the Japanese Government in reply to the message forwarded to that Government by the Secretary of State on August 11. I deem this reply a full acceptance of the Potsdam Declaration which specifies the unconditional surrender of Japan. In the reply there is no qualification.

Arrangements are now being made for the formal signing of surrender terms at the earliest possible moment.

General Douglas MacArthur has been appointed the Supreme Allied Commander to receive the Japanese surrender. Great Britain, Russia, and China will be represented by high-ranking officers.

Meantime, the Allied armed forces have been ordered to suspend offensive action.

The proclamation of V-J Day must wait upon the formal signing of the surrender terms by Japan.

Following is the Japanese Government's message accepting our terms:

"Communication of the Japanese Government of August 14, 1945, addressed to the Governments of the United States, Great Britain, the Soviet Union, and China:

"With reference to the Japanese Government's note of August 10 regarding their acceptance of the provisions of the Potsdam declaration and the reply of the Governments of the United States, Great Britain, the Soviet Union, and China sent by American Secretary of State Byrnes under the date of August 11, the Japanese Government have the honor to communicate to the Governments of the four powers as follows:

"1. His Majesty the Emperor has issued an Imperial rescript regarding Japan's acceptance of the provisions of the Potsdam declaration.

"2. His Majesty the Emperor is prepared to authorize and ensure the signature by his Government and the Imperial General Headquarters of the necessary terms for carrying out the provisions of the Potsdam declaration. His Majesty is also prepared to issue his commands to all the military, naval, and air authorities of Japan and all the forces under their control wherever located to cease active operations, to surrender arms and to issue such other orders as may be required by the Supreme Commander of the Allied Forces for the execution of the above-mentioned terms."

A Bibliographic Review

THE OUTPOURING of writings on World War II continues, and the interested student is advised to begin his investigation by consulting some of the surveys of the literature. Most comprehensive are Louis Morton, *Writings on World War II,* American Historical Association Pamphlet no. 66 (Washington, 1967); and his review article, "World War II: A Survey of Recent Writings," *American Historical Review,* LXXV (December 1970), 1987–2008. The indispensable source for the diplomacy of the war is the multivolume series published by the Department of State, *Foreign Relations of the United States: Diplomatic Papers.* Containing official correspondence, transcriptions of conversations, minutes of meetings, and other documents, these professionally edited and minutely indexed volumes have been appearing approximately twenty-three years after the events they cover. The ordinarily chronological treatment has been supplemented by special volumes on the wartime conferences. For a survey of the series, see Richard W. Leopold, "The Foreign Relations Series: A Centennial Estimate," *Mississippi Valley Historical Review,* XLIX (March 1963), 595–612; and a more detailed account of eighteen volumes covering the early war years may be found in Raymond G. O'Connor, "Foreign Relations of the United States: Diplomatic Papers, 1940–1943: A Review Article," *Pacific Historical Review,* XXXIV (August 1965), 349–58. Another work which must be placed in the category of a "source" is the magisterial six-volume account by Winston Churchill, *The Second World War* (Boston, 1948–53): I, *The Gathering Storm* (1948); II, *Their Finest Hour* (1949); III, *The Grand Alliance* (1950); IV, *The Hinge of Fate* (1950); V, *Closing the Ring* (1951); VI, *Triumph and Tragedy* (1953).

More than a memoir, this work contains the texts of many documents otherwise denied the historian because of Great Britain's thirty-year rule for access to materials in the Foreign Office files. The reader should be aware that the Prime Minister is presenting his version of events, and recall the adage that the best way to make sure of your place in history is to write it yourself. The official British version is Sir Llewellyn Woodward, *British Foreign Policy in the Second World War* (London, 1962), although the author explains that while being allowed access to documents the views expressed are his own. More detailed volumes are scheduled for forthcoming publication.

The diplomatic and military events of the war have been subjected to numerous analyses and a variety of interpretations. Those who challenge the conventional or generally accepted version of the past are termed "revisionists," and ordinarily they are critical of what happened, how it happened, and why it happened. Among the reasons for a reinterpretation of events by historians are plain disagreement with the policy followed, political animosity, the availability of new evidence, and the direction of subsequent events as influenced by previous actions. Revisionists often attempt to point out the difference between the record as presented at the time and the "realities" of the situation as revealed by hitherto undisclosed material, and occasionally they ascribe Machiavellian methods and sinister motives to the leading figures. The revisionist also can exemplify the contention that history must be rewritten by every generation to reflect the interests and aspirations of the age. Changing circumstances, such as the Axis menace's being succeeded by a Communist threat, can modify perspective, and the historian, even though he may strive for objectivity, does not function in a vacuum. In his attempt to describe and explain the past, the historian is an artist, not a scientist—unable to reproduce events in time or in space, employing words as his medium, and seeking original sources for his materials.

Evidence pertaining to prewar diplomacy early became available as a result of the Joint Congressional Committee investigation of the attack on Pearl Harbor, which produced thirty-nine volumes of documents and testimony in 1945 and 1946. Relying heavily on this material, the distinguished American historian Charles A. Beard launched the first major assault on administration policies in his *President Roosevelt and the Coming of the War 1941: A Study in Appearances and Realities* (New Haven, 1948). A sequel to his *American Foreign Policy in the Making, 1932–1940* (New Haven, 1946), this second volume contended that the President deliberately provoked Japan into war in order to bring America into the European struggle. A more elaborate treatment of this theme is followed in Charles C. Tansill, *Back Door to War: The Roosevelt Foreign Policy, 1933–1941* (Chicago, 1952), the author having been allowed to consult many unpublished State Department records. A point-by-point rejection of the Beard thesis appeared in Basil Rauch, *From Munich to Pearl Harbor: A Study in the Creation of a Foreign Policy* (New York, 1950), and the revisionist position was more substantively challenged by the two-volume work of William L. Langer and S. Everett Gleason, *The Challenge to Isolation, 1937–1940* (New York, 1952), and *The Undeclared War, 1940–1941* (New York, 1953). Not uncritical, the authors deny any sort of conspiracy or ulterior motive, as does Herbert Feis in what is the most satisfactory one-volume account of the events, *The Road to Pearl Harbor* (Princeton, 1950). A vigorous defense of policy toward Japan is presented in *The Memoirs of Cordell Hull* (2 vols., New York, 1948), by the secretary of state who conducted most of the negotiations, and his version of this period and the war years should be balanced by the more critical study by Julius W. Pratt, *Cordell Hull* (2 vols., New York, 1964).

Convenient surveys of the Second World War available in paperback are A. Russell Buchanan, *The United States and World War II* (2 vols., New York, 1964), and Gordon Wright, *The Ordeal of Total War, 1939–1945* (New York, 1968), with the latter focusing on the European scene. The fullest and most authoritative single volumes on the diplomacy of the war are Herbert Feis, *Churchill, Roosevelt, and Stalin: The War They Waged and the Peace They Sought* (Princeton, 1957), which is quite detailed and less interpretive; Robert E. Sherwood, *Roosevelt and Hopkins: An Intimate History* (revised edition, New York, 1950), which is distinctly favorable to the President; and William Hardy McNeill, *America, Britain and Russia: Their Co-operation and Conflict, 1941–1946* (London, 1953), which is highly critical of Roosevelt. In the same spirit is the brief study by Gaddis Smith,

American Diplomacy During the Second World War, 1941–1945 (New York, 1965), in which the author faults the President for being too concerned with military affairs and for frustrating Churchill's efforts to restrain Russia. A corrective is John Snell, *Illusion and Necessity: The Diplomacy of Global War, 1939–1945* (Boston, 1963), where Roosevelt appears in a better light. An indispensable source containing addresses, promulgations, excerpts from press conferences, and explanatory material is Samuel I. Rosenman, ed., *The Public Papers and Addresses of Franklin D. Roosevelt*, 13 vols. (New York [vols. 1–5, 1938; vols. 6–9, 1941; vols. 10–13, 1950]). A recent comprehensive study of the President's activities on the domestic as well as the military and diplomatic fronts is James MacGregor Burns, *Roosevelt The Soldier of Freedom* (New York, 1970). Impressively researched, this work is sympathetic yet critical of the President's efforts to achieve a peaceful world. In a short volume of lectures entitled *Roosevelt and World War II* (Baltimore, 1969), Robert A. Divine depicts the President as an isolationist in the 1930s and contends that "Roosevelt's overriding concern for subordinating postwar issues to the immediate task of winning the war" prevented him from achieving his goals. Stressing even more the shortcomings of American policy, William L. Neumann in his *After Victory: Churchill, Roosevelt, Stalin and the Making of the Peace* (New York, 1967), emphasizes Roosevelt's "miscalculations." Taking a somewhat different approach is Gabriel Kolko, *The Politics of War: The World and United States Foreign Policy, 1943–1945* (New York, 1968), in which the author contends that the President was virtually ignorant of the diplomatic realities and allowed his advisers to formulate and implement a hard-line policy toward the Soviet Union, a policy which in their terms was successful.

Politics of War is one of the more recent works produced by what some refer to as the New Left or radical school of historians, who tend to place the blame for the Cold War with Russia on the United States, which, these writers maintain, followed a policy of hostility toward the Soviet Union largely for economic reasons. Capitalist motives dominated the American decision-makers, and the origins of the confrontation with Russia are to be found in World War II military strategy and diplomacy. Gar Alperovitz, in his *Atomic Diplomacy: Hiroshima and Potsdam* (New York,

1965), maintains that the atomic bomb was used not to defeat Japan but to impress the Kremlin with this awesome new weapon and further the Truman anti-communist objectives. Denying any such motive are Herbert Feis, *The Atomic Bomb and the End of World War II* (Princeton, 1966), in which the use of this weapon is considered justified under the circumstances, although not necessary to bring about surrender; and Kolko, *The Politics of War,* cited above. *Beginnings of the Cold War* (Bloomington, Ind., 1966), by Marvin F. Herz, sees the period between the Yalta and Potsdam conferences as crucial, when American recalcitrance virtually forced the Soviet Union to adopt a more aggressive line. Much of this revisionist literature is contained in studies covering more than the war years, such as Denna F. Fleming, *The Cold War and Its Origins, 1917–1960* (2 vols., London, 1961); David Horowitz, ed., *Containment and Revolution* (Boston, 1967); N. D. Houghton, ed., *Struggle Against History: United States Foreign Policy in an Age of Revolution* (New York, 1968); William Appleman Williams, *The Tragedy of American Diplomacy* (2nd ed., New York, 1962); and Lloyd C. Gardner, *Architects of Illusion: Men and Ideas in American Foreign Policy, 1941–1949* (Chicago, 1970). Just when the Cold War began is still a matter of disputation or definition, but most of the revisionists agree that it originated in the context of World War II, and that the United States was largely responsible for its outbreak.

As is apparent from the foregoing, Roosevelt is criticized both for being too hard or too soft on the Russians. In regard to military strategy, incisive critiques are found in Hanson W. Baldwin, *Great Mistakes of the War* (New York, 1950), and Chester Wilmot, *The Struggle for Europe* (New York, 1952), both of which castigate the unconditional surrender policy. The fullest assault on the doctrine is Anne Armstrong, *Unconditional Surrender: The Impact of the Casablanca Policy Upon World War II* (New Brunswick, N.J., 1961), which continues the theme of the two previously mentioned volumes, that Roosevelt was obsessed by military concerns and allowed Russia to gain control of much of Europe. Also critical are Wallace Carroll, *Persuade or Perish* (Boston, 1948), and B. H. Liddell Hart, *History of the Second World War* (New York, 1970), who contends that "the unnecessary prolongation of the Second World War, in pursuit of the op-

ponents' 'unconditional surrender,' proved of profit only to Stalin—
by opening the way for Communist domination of central Europe."
Defending the President are Kent Roberts Greenfield, *American Strategy in World War II: A Reconsideration* (Baltimore, 1961), and Samuel Eliot Morison, *Strategy and Compromise* (Boston, 1958). Supporting the American position are
two persuasive volumes by Trumbull Higgins, *Winston Churchill
and the Second Front, 1940–1943* (New York, 1957), and *Soft
Underbelly: The Anglo-American Controversy over the Italian
Campaign, 1939–1945* (New York, 1968), in which the author
indicates the shortcomings of the British indirect or peripheral
approach.

The military dimensions of the war are admirably presented
in the monumental series United States Army in World War II,
prepared by the Historical Division of the Department of the
Army. Over eighty volumes have appeared so far encompassing
both "grand strategy" and campaigns, all written by professional
historians who were given complete latitude in their interpretations.
Of particular interest to the student of diplomacy are: Mark S.
Watson, *Chief of Staff: Prewar Plans and Preparations* (Washington, 1950); Louis Morton, *The War in the Pacific: Strategy and
Command: The First Two Years* (Washington, 1962); Maurice
Matloff and Edwin S. Snell, *Strategic Planning for Coalition Warfare, 1941–1942* (Washington, 1953); Maurice Matloff, *Strategic
Planning for Coalition Warfare, 1943–1944* (Washington, 1959);
Forrest C. Pogue, *The Supreme Command* (Washington, 1954);
and a book of essays contributed by members of the Historical
Division of the Department of the Army, Kent Roberts Greenfield, ed., *Command Decisions* (Washington, 1960). These works
are among the finest examples of military and "official" history,
thoroughly documented and well written, combining narrative and
analytical qualities of the highest order. The politics of military
strategy has never been more fully portrayed.

To resume with some of the more controversial aspects of
the war, substantial defenses of the unconditional surrender policy
are John L. Chase, "Unconditional Surrender Reconsidered,"
Political Science Quarterly, LXX (June 1955), 258–79; John P.
Glennon, " 'This Time Germany Is a Defeated Nation': The
Doctrine of Unconditional Surrender and Some Unsuccessful At-

tempts to Alter It, 1943–1944," in Gerald N. Grob, ed., *Statesmen and Statecraft of the Modern West: Essays in Honor of Dwight E. Lee and H. Donaldson Jordon* (Barre, Mass., 1967), 109–51; and Paul Kecskemeti, *Strategic Surrender: The Politics of Victory and Defeat* (Stanford, 1958). The latter is a perceptive analysis of the subject, using as case studies the surrenders of France, Italy, Germany, and Japan. Recent appraisals of the German resistance movement are found in *The German Resistance to Hitler: Resistance Thinking on Foreign Policy,* by Hermann Graml; *Social Views and Constitutional Plans of the Resistance,* by Hans Mommsen; *Resistance in the Labour Movement,* by Hans-Joachim Reichardt; *Political and Moral Motives Behind the Resistance,* by Ernst Wolf, Introduction by F. L. Carsten (Berkeley and Los Angeles, 1970), which conclude, in the words of one reviewer, that "the resistance to Hitler's barbarism by decent German citizens was widespread and genuine—and tragically ineffective." A somewhat different version is Hans Rothfels, *The German Opposition to Hitler: An Appraisal* (revised edition, Chicago, 1962), which maintains that the "Casablanca formula" prevented an earlier peace.

The Prime Minister has come in for his share of criticism from his former colleagues and other of his fellow countrymen. Field Marshal Sir Alan Brooke, Chief of the Imperial General Staff, reveals his irritation at Churchill's military strategy in his diaries published in two volumes, Arthur Bryant, ed., *The Turn of the Tide, 1939–1943* (London, 1957), and *Triumph in the West* (London, 1959). Anthony Eden, British Foreign Secretary during much of the war, describes what he considers the Prime Minister's fumbling diplomacy in *The Reckoning* (Boston, 1965). A revealing account with a surprising amount of information on military and diplomatic matters is *Churchill: Taken from the Diaries of Lord Moran* (Boston, 1966), written by the Prime Minister's personal physician. Incisive critiques of Churchill by British historians are two essays in *Churchill Revised: A Critical Assessment* (New York, 1969), Basil Liddell Hart, "The Military Strategist," and A. J. P. Taylor, "The Statesman." A convenient selection of appraisals, both pro and con, is contained in Brian Gardner, *Churchill in Power: As Seen by His Contemporaries* (Boston, 1970).

Certain summit conferences have received special attention. The then Secretary of State, Edward R. Stettinius, Jr., gives a spirited defense of American policies in his *Roosevelt and the Russians: The Yalta Conference* (Garden City, N.Y., 1949), and a more objective but still favorable appraisal is John Snell, ed., *The Meaning of Yalta: Big Three Diplomacy and the New Balance of Power* (Baton Rouge, La., 1956). A recent detailed account of the Crimea meeting that utilizes Russian materials is Diane Shaver Clemens, *Yalta* (New York, 1970). Truman's encounter with Roosevelt's wartime colleagues is described in Herbert Feis, *Between War and Peace: The Potsdam Conference* (Princeton, 1960). An "inside" view of the conferences is provided by the chief of staff to both Presidents Roosevelt and Truman, Fleet Admiral William D. Leahy, in his *I Was There* (New York, 1950), based on his notes and diaries. Earlier, Leahy had served as Chief of Naval Operations and ambassador to the French Vichy government, and he was in charge of the White House "Map Room" where the more important documents were kept. As of 1970 all of these papers were still not available to historians.

The elaborate and intricate planning for the peace is ably presented in the State Department publication, Harley A. Notter, *Postwar Foreign Policy Preparation, 1939–1945* (Washington, 1949), written by one of the participants. Efforts toward American participation in a world body are described in Robert A. Divine, *Second Chance: The Triumph of Internationalism in America During World War II* (New York, 1967). A comprehensive collection of documents is Louise W. Holborn, ed., *War and Peace Aims of the United Nations* (2 vols., Boston, 1943, 1948). The first volume covers the period September 1, 1939–December 31, 1942, and the second January 1, 1943–September 1, 1945. The President's "grand design" is fully expounded in Willard Range, *Franklin D. Roosevelt's World Order* (Athens, Ga., 1959). A popular contemporary book dealing with problems of the postwar world was *Prefaces to Peace* (New York, 1943), labeled a "symposium," and consisting of writings by Wendell L. Willkie, Herbert Hoover and Hugh Gibson, Henry A. Wallace, and Sumner Welles. The interest in these writings by luminaries of diverse political affiliations revealed a widespread concern with the final settlement. In recent years the subject of conflict termination has led to a number of studies, and the student is referred to the "Special Issue on Peace Research in History," of the *Journal of Peace Research in History* (1969, No. 4); and "How Wars End," *The Annals of the American Academy of Political and Social Science* (November 1970). The search for an end to violence in international affairs has been accelerated by the development of more efficient methods of mass destruction, and the challenge remains whether the social sciences and humanities will keep pace with technology.

Index